STAY
THE
COURSE

STAY THE COURSE

A PASTOR'S GUIDE to Navigating
the Restless Waters of Ministry

MIKE MINTER

PUBLISHING
NASHVILLE, TENNESSEE

To the saints at RBC

ACKNOWLEDGMENTS

F ew books are written without the contribution of others, and this book is no exception. One Sunday morning after the service, Erin Brown on our worship team overheard me say I was writing a book. Erin responded with, "I was born with a red pen in my hand." She jumped in with both feet and started scouring the manuscript in search of typos, misspellings, and grammatical errors. She also made valuable suggestions in clarifying the flow of the narrative. Thanks, Erin, for your eagle eye and red pen.

My good friend Travis McSherley and I have worked on other writing projects together. He is a far better writer than I am and has a keen sense of how the reader might interpret what has been written. He pushed me hard and sent me back to my writing desk to rethink and rewrite paragraphs and chapters. Having Travis looking over my shoulder is the coach every writer needs to iron out the wrinkles in the manuscript. He is such a clear thinker, and for that I am most grateful.

CONTENTS

FOREWORD

Mike Minter is one of the most amazing pastors I have ever known. He founded and pastored Reston Bible Church for forty-seven years. Praise God! Through all the ups and downs of ministry, Mike stayed faithful: faithful to God, faithful to his family, faithful to the church, and faithful to his calling. Mike truly stayed the course.

In a day and time when many pastors leave the ministry or are disqualified because of poor choices, Mike has been a model of consistency. Mike's strength is that he has allowed Jesus to radically impact his own personal heart and life. He is a man of tremendous character and integrity. He is humble and kind. He cares more about Jesus and people than he does about himself. Mike has grown RBC into a large church in the Washington, D.C., area. He has impacted government officials and leaders in our world, all with the grace, joy, and humility of Jesus.

It takes a long time for something great to grow. But we live in a society of instant gratification, where the average tenure of a pastor is three or four years. Yet Mike shows us what can happen when we stay the course. This is where long-term growth happens, and this is where generations are impacted. Mike has led people to Christ, discipled them, baptized them, performed their weddings, dedicated their children, and performed their children's weddings. His ministry spans generations.

Mike loves his family. I have the privilege to know his family personally—his wonderful wife, his children, and his grandchildren are all walking with Jesus, and this is so inspiring. His daughter, Kelly, is one of the best women's Bible study teachers in the country. She is fully committed to Jesus, and her dad's love for Scripture is evident in her. All of Mike's children are amazing—they love their dad and Jesus. This is not a guarantee for any pastor—even great pastors can have wayward children. But to observe Mike's family is to observe a man who didn't sacrifice his family on the altar of ministry.

As I write this, I am at a Jungle Pastor's Conference in the middle of the Amazon, a conference Mike founded years ago. His personal passion is to encourage, train, and equip other pastors. Through a ministry called Justice & Mercy International, Mike has been discipling pastors who will take the gospel to the ends of the earth. It is such an honor and a joy to watch him minister to these pastors, many of whom come from all over the Amazon, traveling days by boat, just to come to this conference. They love him. Mike's heart for Jesus and for these pastors is changing the world.

I'm so excited about this book and for the next generation of pastors whom Mike will be pouring into through this writing. Get ready to learn, grow, and gain a heart of wisdom.

We all need wise mentors in our life. We need godly men who have gone before us and can help us navigate the joys and the struggles of life and ministry. Mike has seen it all and done it all. In this book, he shares with us the wisdom and experience we all need.

I'm so thankful for my mentor and friend. Mike has taught me so much personally about ministry, pastoring, and missions, and I know God will teach you so much through this book as well. I pray for more pastors to be like Mike and for our God to raise up pastors and leaders who lead, love, and live like Jesus. Those people will impact churches, generations, and the world for our Savior Jesus Christ. Blessings on Mike, and may the Lord's work through him continue to influence generations of pastors and churches for the glory of our great God!

Jeff Simmons, founder and senior pastor
Rolling Hills Community Church in Nashville, Tennessee

PREFACE

I once read *Open*, the autobiography of the legendary tennis player, Andre Agassi. I don't play tennis, so why would I read his story? Well, because it took me into a world I never knew existed. I learned about string tension, the difference between hard courts and grass courts, and the mental anguish that comes before each tournament. It was all fascinating to me. The experience was palpable. I could practically feel the sweat trickling down my face as I was moments away from hoisting the Wimbledon trophy before thousands of adoring fans. Agassi had me step into his life and feel every throbbing heartbeat of match point.

After that, I read *The Accidental President* by A. J. Baime, a very different book that threw me into the world of Harry S. Truman and the messy universe of politics. It was almost overwhelming to comprehend the apprehension that President Truman felt before giving the green light to bomb Japan with a nuclear device.

Good books, whether fiction or nonfiction, bring readers into unfamiliar environments. What string tension will he use on a grass court? What matrix will be employed to tip the scales in favor of dropping a bomb that will eradicate thousands of lives?

This is a book about pastoral ministry and the local church. It is written for pastors, but not exclusively. I hope it proves valuable for anyone who wishes to peek behind the curtain of ministry, as I did with tennis and politics. It is a book for anyone who has a heart for the local church or is concerned about the lack of unity in the body of Christ. There are wonderful things taking place in the global Church, particularly outside of the United States, but there is also plenty of room for growth. Division is rampant, and the debates that rage among Christians often make Democrats and Republicans look like buddies. It's tragic, really. And it may seem that Christ's prayer that "all of them may be one, Father, just as you are in me and I am in you" (John 17:21) is not even close to being realized.

It is easy to be discouraged as wars are fought among fellow believers. I want pastors to stay the course and be the generation that will be the answer to the Lord's prayer that we would be *one*.

INTRODUCTION

You have probably seen the ads from Farmers Insurance that claim, "We know a thing or two because we've seen a thing or two." Well, after pastoring the same church for nearly fifty years, I know a thing or two because I've seen a thing or two. I humbly acknowledge that I do not have all the answers to ministry challenges, but I do believe I have earned the right to share some thoughts on the subject.

So, after years of teaching and pastoring, I felt it was time to put in writing my reflections about ministry and the Christian life. Through all these decades, there is very little I have not experienced. I've been there and done that. I have seen staff squabbles, congregation problems, elder issues, volunteer challenges, and moral failures. But I have also observed divine appointments, lives transformed by the gospel, families restored, souls saved, and prodigals racing home to receive an embrace of mercy and devour the fatted calf (cf. Luke 15:20–24).

I have been threatened by people who were "told by God" to run me out of town. I've had health problems due to the stress and strain of ministry. But I've also felt the unspeakable pleasure that comes from being an instrument of the Lord's grace. I have had days of victory and days of defeat. I have, at times, cowered under the pressure. I have argued with God and told him what *he* was doing wrong. I have wrestled with demons. I have been praised and maligned. I have been both rightly and falsely accused. The waters of ministry have been both turbulent and calm.

I once grabbed a man just before he tried to kill his wife and mother-in-law, and I have fled like Elijah from Jezebel. I have been publicly applauded and publicly humiliated. I have made good decisions and bad decisions. I have brought healing to people and wounded them as well. I have had friends leave and others stick with me through thick and thin. I've driven people from the Lord and brought people to Christ. I've married people, buried people, counseled people, visited people in hospitals, held the hands of dying children, and held the hands of their grieving parents. I have seen people strengthened by severe adversity and watched others chuck their faith over a lost job. I have had a gun waved in my face, been called a liar, been sneered at, and received harsh, unsigned letters— followed by notes of encouragement that lifted my spirit for another day of battle.

I have been trapped in the jungles of Bolivia, gotten horribly sick in Latvia, and brought back a parasite from Brazil. I have visited the most wretched prisons in Russia and seen cruelty I never dreamed existed. I have been forced out of a bus in the Andes mountains by guerrillas. I've watched the Amazon River rise so high that people's homes were completely submerged and I had to climb through a roof to deliver food and the gospel. I have seen the power of the gospel grip hearts and bring eternity to tribes and tongues in various parts of the world.

I have doubted like Thomas and had the faith of Daniel. I have been at war with myself, with God, and with my faith, only to rise and find peace and rest in his matchless gospel. I have been angry with my congregation and have loved them with the love of Christ. I have preached in the flesh one weekend and been led by the Spirit the next. I have felt powerful in my own strength before approaching the pulpit and then experienced the sour fruit of what man produces. Then I have come in the next week broken, only to witness God do "great and mighty things, which you do not know" (Jer. 33:3 NKJV).

I have been called a legalist, a heretic, and a Bible-thumper. Some have told me that I'm warm and approachable, while others chide me for being cold and indifferent. Some have yelled at me while others embraced me tightly. I have been stabbed in the back by some and had my wounds tended by others. I have been called a total failure, and I have been exalted in ways of which I am not deserving.

I have held firmly to secondary doctrines only to change my mind later. I have been blessed with the gift of communicating God's truth, but I have also misrepresented him when I've leaned on my own understanding. I have dedicated babies and then years later officiated their weddings. I have been lifted up with pride and humbled by the One who deserves all the preeminence. I have defended myself, and I have often realized how futile that was.

I have given good counsel and bad counsel. I have had to sail the stormy waters of four suicides and a murder within our church body (all within just a fifteen-month period). I have run the ship aground a few times over the years and brought her through some of the roughest seas. I have come to realize that when all is well, you give God the glory, and when mistakes are made, you shoulder the blame.

Does any of this strike a chord? Whether you are fresh out of seminary or have been pastoring for decades, you've probably experienced many of the glorious mountaintops and difficult valleys that come with this calling. My hope and prayer is that through the pages of this book, you might gain some encouragement or insight from a fellow sojourner who has been walking this path for a long time.

This book is divided into two sections. First, I will give you a brief overview of my story. I will share how I came to know Christ, how the Lord led me to plant a church in Northern Virginia, and how he has built and grown our church in the years since.

In the second part, I will offer a glimpse into the unvarnished truth of the world of ministry. I will share what the Lord has shown me during my decades of ministry and offer counsel, exhortation, and warnings that I trust will be a benefit to you. We will look at the unique burdens, temptations, and joys that come with being a pastor. We will navigate the turbulent waters of criticism, doubt, and discouragement. And we will ask the Lord to help us stay the course to the end, that we might leave a legacy of faithfulness and hear our God say, "Well done."

So I invite you to climb aboard and enjoy this journey with me.

PART 1

CHAPTER 1

MY STORY

Mike Minter! What in the world are you doing?"

The words echoed louder than the golf cleats hitting the marble counter. Those words, and those shoes, did not belong to one of the members of the country club. They weren't the shoes of Bea Smith, whose usual greeting was much more cordial. Neither did I hear the accompanying sound of change or the unfolding of a dollar bill that was the standard payment for my services. Just that jolting question: "Mike Minter, what in the *world* are you doing?"

I looked up slowly, but there was no way to hide my embarrassment. The redness of my face displayed the humiliation of my soul.

As it turned out, the man who handed me his shoes was an old classmate of mine, Joe, from my days at the United States Naval Academy. We had entered Annapolis in the early 1960s, and as plebes (freshmen), we had shined countless pairs of shoes. Joe served his mandatory four years as a marine and then left the military for a career in real estate. And I chose a different route, as you'll soon see.

Joe had become quite successful and now owned a beautiful home not far from the club, while I struggled to make the rent for my one-bedroom apartment. So what was I doing shining shoes? How would I feel if he left me a tip? How would he feel about giving me one?

I finally confessed that I had just moved to Northern Virginia to start a church. Imagine how I felt telling an old college buddy, who was now a real estate tycoon, that I was shining shoes in order to put food on the table so I could start a conservative church in a liberal community. Did he have a clue what I was talking about, or did I seem to be a miserable failure trying to cover up my lowly state by manufacturing some story about church planting? Should I have cared what he thought? Whether or not I should have cared, I did.

What in the world *was* I doing? As we begin our journey, I want to spend a few chapters providing a brief autobiographical sketch, so that you can get to know me and understand my motives for writing this book.

You see, Pastor, I already know you. I know you well. I know your pain and disillusionment. If you're just beginning your ministry, I know your idealism, your hopes, your dreams, as well as your fears. If you've been around a while, I know your discouragement and the criticism you have endured. I know what your wife has experienced and how your children have felt. I know of the endless meetings you have endured, many of them going far differently than expected. I know the one-on-one breakfasts you've had with members of the body who have revealed to you the latest rumblings about your leadership style. Yes, I know—oh, how I know.

In the 1800s, Anglican bishop J. C. Ryle said, "Give me a candle and a Bible and shut me up in a dark dungeon, and I will tell you everything that the whole world is doing."[1] Allow me to piggyback on it: Give me nearly fifty years as a pastor, lock me in a dungeon, and I will tell you what pastors everywhere are experiencing. Since the Lord has graciously granted me several decades as a pastor in the same church, I can tell you what you have already experienced or will experience along the journey, and the blessings and trials promised by Scripture to all who wish to advance the kingdom.

My supreme desire at this stage of my life and ministry is to shepherd the shepherds. I want to put my arm around your shoulder and walk you through every bewildering situation and help you rejoice in the blessings of changed lives. I trust this book will be a companion and mentor as you travel this lonely road. We will meet difficult people along the way, deal with criticism, experience false accusations, feel the pain of a cracked whip upon the back of our reputation, sense the bite of a sarcastic comment just before we enter the pulpit, and, perhaps the most hurtful, lose good friends for bad reasons.

But we will also focus on the joy that comes through advancing God's kingdom and seeing lives changed. There will be the double-edged sword of the "thrill of victory and the agony of defeat." We will learn how to preach when we don't feel like it and how to draw from the well of grace, which will be needed to keep on keeping on. These initial chapters will serve as a reference point as you read the rest of the book. I intend to be brutally honest about who I am—the good, the bad, and the ugly. I want to help keep you on the front lines and not among those who resign in despair or burnout. I want your marriage to be strong so that you won't join the tragic group of pastors who fall into divorce or adultery. No, we must be men who are faithful to our call. If this book in any way helps you do that, all praise to God.

Growing Up Years

Before I take you on a deep dive regarding my academic career (and I *did* make it a career), I thought it might be beneficial to give you a brief biographical sketch of my early years. I was born in Providence, Rhode Island, just prior to the end of World War II. My father was a naval officer who graduated from the U.S. Naval Academy in 1937 with a passion for flying. My earliest memories go back to when we were stationed in Hawaii in the early fifties. Twice my dad was sent into the Korean War for nine-month periods, and my mom had to hold down the fort at home.

Many years later, it was obvious that my dad was on the fast track as a naval officer. In the early sixties, he was the skipper of the USS *Intrepid*, an aircraft carrier that is now a museum stationed in New York. He later became Commandant of the Naval Academy and eventually Superintendent, which was equivalent to being president of a major university. In my late teens, we moved into the 17,000-square-foot Superintendent's quarters located on the Naval Academy's campus. This incredible home afforded me access to a life that few people ever experience. Presidents, senators, congressmen, dignitaries from around the world, and entertainers all visited our home. One day I came down for lunch and sat next to Billy Graham, who was the visiting speaker for the Protestant chapel service. I saw Senator Ted Kennedy and his wife Joan wandering around the quarters one afternoon. As you can see, my childhood was far from ordinary.

Despite my unusual upbringing, my religious mother made sure her three children were in church every week. This is where I learned about God and Christ and how to live a moral life. But it wasn't until the age of twenty-six that I discovered Jesus was my Savior. I will share more about that discovery later.

CHAPTER 2

THE ELUSIVE "A"

Mike, do you understand what the class is doing?"

I can still see my kindergarten teacher standing over my desk, asking me this question. After some minor academic exercise, she had gone around the room, looking over the students' shoulders and encouraging them on their work. "Nice work, Johnny!" "Sally, that's terrific!"

But when she observed my efforts, she spoke those innocent words that would be said to me by teachers and administrators throughout my academic career. That question played over and over in my mind during all of my school years: "Mike, do you understand what the class is doing?"

Back in 1954, when my brother was in the ninth grade, he came home with straight A's on his report card. We had a family reunion at the time and everyone chipped in a few bucks in honor of his achievement. He walked away with $36, which, in those days, felt like a fortune. I knew that I would never receive such a prize. I don't recall feeling jealous of my brother's reward, but it did sting to know that if grades were the measurement for financial success, I would never see a dime.

At this point, you might think I am being dramatic. After all, many of you might remember going through a year of school without earning an A. Some of you might even admit to going two or three years without bringing an A home. I, however, managed to go through nineteen and a half years of education without ever seeing a single A etched onto my report card.

Yes, you read that right: *nineteen and a half years* with no A's. Most folks require five years of grade school, three years of middle school, and four years of high school, which totals twelve. If you throw in four years of college, that is sixteen. I took a more circuitous route.

In the ninth grade at Granby High School in Norfolk, Virginia, I opened up my final report card to find *straight F's,* the opposite of *straight A's.* I didn't pass a single class—nothing, zero. Instead of $36, I was gifted another tour of the ninth grade.

My mom didn't worry about it at all. She always said to me, "You're just going to wind up on stage someday." (She was convinced that I was going to be a stand-up comedian.) But it was really hard on my dad, a three-star admiral and Superintendent of the Naval Academy. I knew it hurt him so much to have a son who just struggled and struggled. Still, he never chided me and always tried to encourage me.

By my junior year of high school, my parents were becoming quite concerned, so they decided to have my IQ tested. Off we went to Stevens Institute of Technology in Hoboken, New Jersey. My dad, in particular, wanted to know, "What's wrong with my son? Why can't he understand directions? Why is everything upside down and confusing?"

I endured a lengthy battery of tests for nearly two days. I remember that the counselor didn't tell me what my IQ was, but he did say, "You have the least ability to visualize of anybody we've ever tested. You have no ability to see something in different dimensions. You can't picture what something would look like in a different place."

Then he said, "I'm going to give you one bit of advice: Stay away from tools."

I took that advice to heart. You should see my tool chest at home. I've got a screwdriver and a wrench—that's it. And I've never used them. To this day, I'm not sure what a hammer looks like or where to plug it in.

Finally, I made it to my senior year of high school—at age nineteen. Though I was inches from the finish line, I was told that I didn't have enough credits to graduate. But then I got a last-minute lift from Mr. Kesmodel, our principal, who—bless his heart—had mercy on me and smuggled in the credits needed for graduation. I'm not sure how he pulled that off, but if he hadn't, I would have graduated from high school as a twenty-year-old.

As we were preparing to attend the commencement ceremony, my father called me into his study and said, "Mike, are you sure you are graduating today?"

His question stung, but I knew he was concerned that I might show up at graduation and find that the name "Minter" would not be called, while the rest of my classmates would march proudly across the stage receiving their diplomas, accompanied by loud cheers. I put my dad's mind at ease by letting him know of the credits that had magically appeared. I still hadn't brought home that A, but I did bring home a diploma.

Cognitive Delay

Before we move on to the journey of my life after high school, I want to give you a quick peek into the inner workings of my brain and the unique challenges that come with it. Rest assured, my openness in this area should not be interpreted as an appeal for pity. This is not my way of saying, "Woe is me," nor is it an invitation to sympathy, cloaked in humility. My struggles have revealed God's grace in ways I never could have anticipated. I have had a great life, filled with blessings and adventure, and the Lord has provided many close friends who have seen me through some of my learning disabilities. I am grateful for a host of companions who help me with my finances, navigation, and complex computer issues like opening up an "email thread" (whatever that is). I have no idea what a "hashtag" is, and I'm not sure I even want to know.

It wasn't until I reached my seventies that the pieces of the puzzle of my mind began to fall into place. As I began to look back over the course of my life, I realized I had found ways to compensate for my weaknesses. I developed a sense of humor—as I mentioned, my mother thought I was destined for a career in comedy—and I discovered verbal skills that would distract people from noticing my deficiencies. Looking back, these coping strategies proved very useful in securing various jobs.

After college, I remember applying for two jobs in which I was told there were many applicants but only one or two openings. This might surprise you, but it never entered my mind that I would not be selected, because I knew that my people skills, coupled with my verbal abilities, meant I couldn't lose. Sure enough, I was offered both jobs. The bigger question I would now face was whether or not I would understand the job. Getting through the door was one thing; becoming comfortable in the room was quite another.

Several years ago, I diagnosed myself with "cognitive delay." I think I coined that term, but perhaps it's a real one. Nevertheless, I use it to describe one of my core struggles: my mind is always about two or three seconds behind the rest of the crowd.

The complications associated with this delay cannot be fully understood unless you have lived with it for a lifetime. A two-second delay while driving at 60 miles per hour means you just missed the turn, and now you have to backtrack, sometimes on a toll road, where you pay three times instead of once. It means you panic when there are cars behind you and you are not sure what the sign says, so you slow down to give your brain a chance to catch up. This results in a line of frustrated motorists who are now leaning on their horns and making you feel stupid because everyone else knows exactly what to do. And then comes a flashback to kindergarten: "Mike, do you understand what the class is doing?"

When I watch a television show with my wife, we have to hit the pause button so she can explain what's going on because the plot is just too fast for me to keep up. Note that I'm talking about Hallmark movies here—not *The Crown*.

A cognitive delay, coupled with an inability to visualize, creates enormous difficulties. When I have to go into a parking garage, I experience mild trauma because I know that in order to leave, there are two functions I must perform correctly for the gate to open. First, I will have to insert the ticket exactly the right way, and second, I must insert my credit card exactly the right way. Upside down or backwards won't do. There is usually a helpful picture that shows the driver how to execute this elementary task. No problem at all for the average Joe. But for *moi*, this is an intense cognitive exercise, and you either pass or fail. There are no points for effort, and there is no middle ground where the gate opens halfway. Plus, there is a time limit on this exam because if I don't move quickly enough, an impatient line will begin to form behind me.

A few years ago, I attended a meeting in a crowded downtown area where I was forced to park in a parking garage. I spent a good bit of time during the meeting thinking about how I would get out of the garage. Who does that? No one, that's who. When the moment came, I gave myself a little pep talk: *Mike, you can do this!*

I first waited to make sure there would be no one behind me. Finally, with all the bravery of a soldier heading into combat, I fired up the engine of my brown Datsun. I backed the car out, approached the pay station, and stared down my nemesis. Carefully, I inserted the ticket and took a deep breath. The flashing red light reminded me that I am not like most people. I froze and prepared to try again. I studied the picture showing how the card was supposed to be inserted, but my visualization skills just couldn't interpret it. The red light flashed relentlessly as if to say, "What's wrong with you? A child can do this!"

I looked in my rearview mirror and saw a man behind me. When you have lived with this all your life, the pride of asking for help must be dismissed or you will be paralyzed every time you leave the house. So I rolled down my window and, with a loud voice, asked if he could help. He got out of his car and briskly walked up to the meter. I explained my dilemma and probably told him I was from Siberia or something, which he would have had no trouble believing. He inserted the ticket. Green light. He inserted my credit card. Another green light. The gate acknowledged that the test was passed and immediately stood at attention, as if to salute his brilliance and my ignorance. Off I went, thanking him profusely. Perhaps, as Hebrews tells us, "thereby some have entertained angels unawares" (Heb. 13:2 KJV).

But my challenges don't stop there. I also interpret directions and signs differently than others. This isn't dyslexia. Words appear to me just fine; I just interpret them differently. My problem is a mixture of cognitive delay, an inability to visualize, and some serious interpretation issues. There have been times when I have literally pulled off the side of the road and said, "Lord, why am I so different from everybody else? Why am I the only one who doesn't understand this? I just don't get it. I try to read the signs, and they just don't say the same thing to me."

For example, when I was in school, exams were a never-ending reminder that I was not like the rest of the class. They served as reinforcements to the notion that there was something wrong with my ability to think. That I saw the world through a different set of glasses. In taking a true-or-false test, I would find ways in which either answer could be correct. On a multiple-choice test, I would come up with other choices that weren't listed. My mind was like a wide-angle lens that captured all possibilities. I rarely see things as black and white, but as more of a smoky gray.

Such tests always took me into a world of social discomfort. While the rest of the class was turning to page three, I would still be trying to figure out what the instructions meant. And listening to post-test remarks from my classmates was painful.

"Boy, that was a piece of cake!"

"Yeah, I raced right through it, but I'm not certain whether I got number two right."

Not sure if you got number *two* right? I wasn't certain I got the directions right, never mind the correct answers. Again, I hear that voice from long ago: "Mike, do you understand what the class is doing?"

These cognitive disabilities have traveled with me all through life. They accompany me in the grocery store, where I read the price labels wrong and pay twice as much as I was prepared to pay. But I dare not embarrass myself by challenging the manager, which I have done in the past, only to be proven wrong. Every form at a doctor's office is filled out wrong. While I request a new one, I continually come up with new excuses to cover my inabilities. I am plagued during meetings where budgets and plans are laid out. I just can't keep up, so I will check out and dream of chasing butterflies on a sunny day. Then when someone asks me later what was decided at the meeting, I don't have a clue. Even assembling a simple toy requires asking a neighbor to come over and assist. But in reality, they end up taking over the job while I do the assisting. "Insert metal flange into collar of beveled edge as shown in Figure 1." What?!

My family is somewhat aware that all of this is going on, and some of my close friends have seen tidbits here and there. However, nobody really knows what I go through on a daily basis. I recently started writing down at the end of the day the number of things I did that nobody else would ever do. It usually ends up being at least five or six. Just a few days ago, I decided to use Google Maps to see if I had been taking the best way home from church. My cognitive delay kicked in big time as I made four wrong turns, which turned a twenty-minute drive into a forty-minute drive.

If it wasn't so funny, I would probably cry. Again, my desire in sharing this with you isn't to elicit pity or make excuses for my shortcomings, but rather to encourage you and point you to a benevolent and powerful God who cannot be thwarted by our weaknesses.

The Naval Academy

To follow up my illustrious high school career, I figured that the most natural thing to do would be to apply to the U.S. Naval Academy. "Wait just a minute," you might say. "How could a man who never earned an A and failed the ninth grade think he could get accepted into one of the most competitive and prestigious schools in our nation? How could someone who had no idea how to figure out his gas mileage, expect to enter a school where only the cream of the crop is accepted? How could a future stand-up comedian find a place in a school that leans heavily on a math and science curriculum and requires high SAT scores?"

Well, after one year of college at Randolph-Macon College in Ashland, Virginia (and still no A's), I decided to apply anyway. As I have mentioned, my dad was the Superintendent of the Academy, and I well remember him trying to talk me out of applying. He knew that I would not get in, and he didn't want me to go through another academic rejection. He also knew that if, by some miracle, I did get in, I would never be able to keep up with the rigorous academic demands, coupled with all of the physical hazing. But I applied anyway, and one fine day an envelope arrived with my name on it from the admissions office at USNA. I opened it and read the word "Congratulations." Without reading any further, I knew I had made the cut.

How I was admitted remains a mystery. To my knowledge, no one in the history of the school had ever been accepted with such a dismal academic background. Obviously, there really is no mystery: someone on the selection committee saw the name "Minter" and said, "This is Admiral Minter's son," and stamped "accepted" on my application without a second thought. There is no other explanation. Fear must have struck my dad's heart when he found out I was going to enter his alma mater.

In June of 1964, the day of reckoning arrived, and the new class was sworn in. What in the world was I doing? I had shown up to the Daytona 500 with a skateboard. I was a 120-pound linebacker in the NFL. I was a five-foot center in the NBA. Valences in chemistry, stress loads in engineering, equations in calculus—I was at the deep end of the pool and I didn't know how to swim. I couldn't breathe. There was no oxygen (which has a valence of eight, by the way). I was in the middle of a foreign land and didn't know a word of the native language.

If those word pictures don't make my situation apparent enough, my grades should make it crystal clear. When the first midterm grades came out, I was the proud owner of a 0.56 grade point average out of a 4.0. Three F's and two D's.

One day on my way to class, I complained to one of my classmates about how hard Academy classes were. He was quick to reply, "Are you kidding? This place is easy."

To which I countered, "Oh yeah, what did you get on your midterms?"

Of the 1,000 freshmen I could have queried, little did I realize I was addressing the man who would stand *numero uno* at graduation, be selected as a Rhodes Scholar, and eventually wear the uniform of a four-star admiral. We did have one thing in common: neither of us had ever gotten a B. God has a great sense of humor.

To add insult to injury, it was customary at meals for the upperclassmen to ask the freshmen how they did on midterms and finals: "2.6, sir!" "3.4, sir!" As they came down the line, beads of sweat, birthed from embarrassment and shame, formed on my brow. When they got to me, I muttered, "0.56, sir."

A fog of silence suddenly descended over the meal. Everyone at the table was stunned. The Superintendent's son had just revealed that the only way someone with such low grades could have gotten into the Academy was if some strings were pulled by the top brass. I never asked my dad what he thought or how he felt, but I knew the word spread like a prairie fire throughout the brigade of midshipmen. It must have kept him and my mom up for nights on end.

At the end of the year, I went before the academic review board and was told I had two choices: I could leave the Academy, or I could repeat my plebe year (minus the hazing). I chose the latter.

During my second plebe year, I obviously had to repeat most of the classes that had to do with math, chemistry, and physics. However, I did not have to repeat English, which meant that I found myself with sophomores and juniors in Professor Rose's English class. One day, the professor announced that each of us would have to deliver a ten-minute speech on one of the traditions at the Academy. We were instructed to be aware of eye contact and to stick to our time limit. We could use 3 x 5 cards for notes. Since my name began with M, it seemed logical that if he went in alphabetical order, I probably had a few weeks to think about it. Drowning in formulas and equations, a ten-minute talk was the least of my worries.

While on my way to English class one day, I suddenly realized I hadn't been keeping track of who might be called on next. What if it was my turn? I would once again look stupid, and with my name tag on my shirt, there was no hiding who I was—Admiral Minter's son.

I quickly remembered some details about one of the statues on Academy grounds, but could I elaborate on that for ten minutes? Sure enough, Professor Rose pointed his gaze right at me. "Mr. Minter, you're up."

I could practically feel the anticipation of the class, as the most recognized name in the student body for academic incompetence was about to reveal his reputation in a public forum. I sauntered up to the front and took a good look at the mammoth IBM clock hanging on the back wall. Ten minutes was all I needed to land this plane. So I did what I have always done best—ad lib. I had not practiced. I had no 3 x 5 cards. I took a breath, announced my subject matter, and launched into my presentation. I did not have to worry about looking down at my notes because I had none.

I paced back and forth, made eye contact, and stared at all those brilliant students as if to say, "Let me show you how this is done." I hit the ten-minute mark and closed it out. Excuse my pride, but like a gymnast sticking a dismount, I knew I had nailed it. Verbalizing my thoughts in an organized manner has always been my way of compensating for all my struggles. Professor Rose looked at the class and said, "Gentlemen, *that's* how you give a speech."

I got an A. It was just for that speech and not my final grade, but I must say it really felt good. This small victory was actually a pivotal point in my life, as I realized that I could stand before a crowd and deliver a speech with little or no preparation. It was a foretaste of what I would be doing for nearly fifty years of my life.

The Scandal

Not long after that accomplishment, I was hit with one of the hardest things I have ever had to endure. I was in a Spanish class and failing. Nothing new there, except that almost everyone in the class was failing as well. The new

Superintendent, who succeeded my dad, was informed of the situation and called in the professor to find out why the class was failing. The professor accused the Superintendent of favoritism because the son of his old pal Admiral Minter was in the class. The professor threatened to report the incident to the press—and then, in fact, followed through with his threat. The Superintendent himself called me on the phone to inform me of the situation. He told me to brace myself because the press was going to have a heyday, since the Academy was a military institution backed by the taxpayers.

The following day, the story was on the front page of the *Washington Post*. It then made its way into *Time* and *Newsweek* magazines, and even Walter Cronkite and David Brinkley reported it on the evening news. There I was again, on center stage, with all of the midshipmen given new material to examine my life with a microscope, provided by the media at no charge. This was just one more piece of evidence that I was getting special treatment because of my father. The molehill was now officially a mountain.

There was nowhere to hide. My mom and dad were overseas with a new assignment. There were no cell phones, text messages, or emails in those days, of course, but I knew that my parents were well aware of the situation. How could they not be, since it was all over the news? My dad had such a great reputation of integrity, that no one who knew him well could have believed he was trying to encourage his successor to aid me by applying academic favoritism. My parents never addressed this situation with me. They just said they were proud of me and we moved on with life. Still, I couldn't help but feel their embarrassment as they mingled with colleagues who must have been treating them awkwardly or asking them all kinds of questions. I kept thinking, *When will this end?*

The answer to that question was delivered by the academic review board in May 1968. I was carrying a 1.97 GPA (on a 4.0 scale) at the end of my fourth year—which was actually my junior term, since I had repeated my plebe year. The board informed me that as a senior, I would be facing the giants of thermodynamics and fluid mechanics. They felt I couldn't take the heat in thermo and would drown in fluids, and, if I'm honest, I knew there was no way I could rise to the challenge.

So after four long years, I was dismissed from the Academy. I thanked the board and they wished me well. I went across the hall to the men's room and found an empty stall where I cried my eyes out.

Still no A.

Before we leave my Academy days, I want to make it very clear that, in spite of everything that transpired, those were some of the best days of my life. I met lifelong friends and am indebted to many classmates who stuck with me through thick and thin. I was glad to know that those were the men who would go on to protect our nation.

One of my greatest regrets is not being able to graduate with them. I would have loved to toss my hat into the air at graduation. I would have loved to have worn the USNA ring. I would have loved to serve my country. Yet it soon became clear that God had a different course for my life.

CHAPTER 3

LIFE AFTER THE ACADEMY

After nineteen and a half years of school, I finally captured the elusive A.

Following my time at the Academy, I transferred my credits to Old Dominion University in Virginia and graduated from there. When I received the final grade of my final class of my final year, there it was—an A in speech class. I know that speech is more of a talent, and it does not require great mental acuity. It is more like being able to run fast or sing well. So it may not be the same as getting an A in physics or history, but it was still an A. In fact, it was the A I had longed for all my life, and it ended up defining my life. As you already know, I would eventually stand before people and speak on a regular basis. I am not sure my congregation would give me an A, but they are very kind in telling me I do a good job.

I have to wonder whether my parents ever contemplated getting one of those bumper stickers where you boast of your kid's achievements? *Proud Parents of an Honor Student. Proud Parents of an Athlete.* Well, how about this one: *Proud Parents of a Son Who Took Nineteen and a Half Years of School to Get an A.*

I am kidding, but my parents really were the greatest. They never said things like, "You won't amount to anything," or, "Why can't you be more like your brother and sister?" They poured endless hours of encouragement into my life. My cup runneth over.

Enter Jesus

After graduation, a friend of mine from the Academy suggested we take a trip to Europe and do some traveling. Bruce had just gotten back from Vietnam, and with his four years of military obligation completed, he had some time on his hands as he pondered what his future might be.

While we traveled from one European country to another, he handed me a copy of the New Testament and asked me to read the Gospel of John. I had never looked inside a Bible in my life. Bruce acted as if he knew God personally. He exemplified the truth that the gospel is best communicated when the conviction of those who believe it can be observed by those who don't. Like a magnet, I was drawn to his life. It was clear that he knew a God with whom I was unfamiliar.

The first evidence of his life-changing relationship with the Almighty came when we arrived in Paris by train. We had purchased a Eurail pass, which allowed us to go anywhere we wanted in Europe for one month. However, we had not made any reservations for lodging and had no idea where we would sleep that night. The information booth was closed, and it was already a few minutes after midnight.

I can get a bit worked up in these kinds of uncertain conditions, so I began complaining. "What are we going to do? Where are we going to sleep tonight?"

Bruce stopped right there in the station and began to pray as though he had a personal hotline to "The Big Guy." He had no sooner come to "Amen" when the lady running the booth arrived on the scene. She had forgotten some important papers and had returned to get them. We asked her if there were any rooms available in the city. She said something to the effect of, "You're in luck. There is a room just around the corner."

This kind of "luck" happened many times throughout the month in Europe. As I look back, I believe God wanted me to see what it looked like for someone to have a real relationship with him—a relationship built on faith and trust in his presence and goodness. Bruce seemed to know the Lord with an intimacy that I didn't think was even possible.

About this time, the Frisbee had grown in popularity in the United States, but it had yet to be introduced in Europe. Prior to leaving for our trip, Bruce and I had spent many hours honing our Frisbee skills, and I must admit that we were pretty good. Each of us had some athletic prowess, and this new invention was a way of showing off before crowds. We traveled to Spain and went out to the beaches tossing this strange flying saucer to the amazement of the locals. Everyone wanted a chance to test their skills to see if they could make this piece of plastic take flight. They soon discovered it was not as easy as it looked.

As we moved closer to Scandinavia, we displayed our new toy at the Tivoli Gardens amusement park in Copenhagen, Denmark. We loved showing off, so we held nothing back. Behind-the-back tosses, under-the-leg catches—the passersby were utterly enthralled.

But finally, we put the Frisbee aside and focused on more important matters of discussion. I finished the Gospel of John, which I read with gusto, and it left me with many questions. I had always understood the concept of "salvation" to be dependent on me being a good person, with a sprinkling of Jesus mixed in. I believed that if I went to church and behaved myself, I could just present my spiritual letter sweater on judgment day. The Lord would be so impressed at my moral life that he would swing the pearly gates wide open at my arrival.

Many religious people think this way. In the back of their minds, they envision a "goodness chart" with the really bad people on one side and the really good people on the other side. To them, they may be somewhere in the middle but are definitely good enough to make the cut. But what if the requirement is that you have to be as good as Mother Teresa or Billy Graham? How can we even know how good is good enough?

Imagine you are preparing for college. You will pay $50,000 per year and plan on working hard on your studies, but you are given zero knowledge of the grading system. The letter of acceptance merely stated that at the time of graduation, you will be told whether you passed or failed. Who in their right mind would spend all that time and money with no idea of whether or not their work would be accepted? It would be a huge gamble for even the best of students. What if it takes a 3.5 GPA to graduate? What if it takes a 3.9?

Yet religious people take this kind of gamble on a daily basis. Eternity is hanging in the balance, but all they can do is hope that their righteous deeds will be satisfactory on judgment day.

Before my trip to Europe with Bruce, I held the same philosophy. I thought I was good enough to make the cut and be accepted into heaven, but how could I know for sure? As Bruce and I talked, I soon learned that the Lord didn't just ask for a few good deeds to enter heaven—he required perfection. Heaven is a perfect place and not even a lie can enter (Rev. 21:27 NKJV). So how can someone ever achieve perfection? That is a good question. It was certainly the question on my heart that night in Copenhagen.

Here is the answer that Bruce gave me: he explained that my eternal salvation had nothing to do with my good behavior, church membership, tithing, or church attendance. So in a bed-and-breakfast in Denmark in June 1970, I discovered the life-altering truth that Christ is my perfection. I stopped trying to earn my salvation and instead accepted what Jesus had accomplished in his death and resurrection. He placed his perfect righteousness to my account. I realized that salvation was not a combination of my good works plus Christ. It was *all* Christ. That same night, I bowed my head and called upon Jesus to save my soul. He did, and my life was turned upside down. No, actually, for the first time, it was right-side up.

As we headed back toward the United States, Bruce grew tired of me complaining about three things: that I had no job, no place to stay, and no money. What I viewed as huge obstacles, he saw as huge opportunities for me to grow in my young faith. Finally, he took the bull by the horns and really started discipling me in life and in the Word. And an excited bull I was. I relished every new piece of understanding that was revealed to me about God's kingdom and my eternal destiny. I became a witnessing machine. If it moved, I was ready to tell it about Jesus.

I returned to America a new man—but a man who still had no job or money. So I decided it was time to get serious about pursuing a career. Florida seemed like a good place to venture into this new life. Bruce exhorted me to find a replacement mentor in Florida, as he knew that I desperately needed encouragement to continue to grow in my faith.

Upon moving to the Sunshine State, I entered the world of life insurance. One afternoon, as I was leaving our office to head home, I noticed a new face. She was a young lady who was hired to answer the phones after hours. I observed her reading her Bible, and I stopped to introduce myself and comment on the Scriptures. She looked up at me and asked, "If you died today, where would you spend eternity?" I told her I was a new believer and had recently trusted Christ.

Having established our mutual identity in Jesus, I told her I was looking for an apartment, and she readily gave me the name of one of her classmates, Rudy, who was attending the nearby Florida Bible College. She also invited me to attend a concert at the college. The night of the concert, I noticed a bulletin board with a list of evening courses. One of the courses offered was on the authority of Scripture. That captured my attention since I knew virtually nothing about this sacred book.

Thus, a simple conversation with a new coworker changed the trajectory of my life forever. When I met Rudy, I knew I had found someone who would become a lifelong friend. I started taking night classes and began a Bible study with Rudy. He wanted to start an evangelistic Bible study for adults, but he had no contacts in the secular world—which is where I came in. My job was to invite nonbelievers to the study, and he would do the teaching. Many people trusted in Christ over the next few months, but then the hatchet fell. Rudy pulled me aside one day and informed me that he was graduating in a few months and would be moving to the other side of the state. "Mike, I need you to take over the study."

Excuse me? I had just come to know the Lord six months earlier, and now I was supposed to be a Bible study leader? I didn't even know where Genesis was located.

The time quickly came when I was to give a message and begin leading the group. Now, I have no recollection of the heresy taught that night, but here is what I do remember: on my way home, in my little Volkswagen Beetle, I heard God say to me, "I want you to leave the world of business and teach the Bible the rest of your life." It wasn't an audible voice, but it was just as clear. I followed those instructions and entered Florida Bible College in 1972, at the age of twenty-eight. I must hold a Guinness World Record for the most freshman years!

The Ministry Journey Begins

In the summer of 1972, I went on a blind date with a young lady named Kay who was attending a Bible college and passionate about ministry. After a few months of dating, she made it abundantly clear she would never marry anyone who didn't intend to be a pastor. Talk about pressure! I had already planned on a life in ministry but had no idea I would meet someone with the same desire. Kay and I fell in love, but as the days went by, she was still a little uncertain. So in my young and foolish attempt to "close the deal," I took a verse out of context. I have no guilt for such manipulation. (Remember, I was a new believer!) I told her that Psalm 37:4 says to "delight in the LORD, and he will give you the desires of your heart." Since I was delighting in the Lord and she was my desire, what else could she say except "I do"? Out of context or not, I guess it worked, for we married in April 1973. I was one month shy of turning twenty-nine, while she was twenty-one. And here we are at the time of writing this with four children and six grandchildren.

I enrolled at Florida Bible College in 1972 as a freshman while Kay was a senior, even though I am almost eight years older than she is. At that time, Florida Bible College was a large school. In the daily chapel service, there were approximately 1,500 students present. One day in 1973, at the end of the service, a man named Mike Schaeffer announced, "Can I see Mike Minter after chapel?" I knew I hadn't done anything wrong, but I couldn't imagine what this was about.

I went up to Mike and he told me, "I know that you and Kay want to go to Virginia. There is a man there named Charlie Swift from a place called Reston, and you may want to just give him a call." Kay and I honeymooned in Virginia and had been thinking about moving to Charlottesville to plant a church.

Charlie worked for Gulf Oil, which was headquartered in Reston at the time. As his job took him from place to place, he would recruit students from Florida Bible College to come join or start a church near him. So I picked up the phone and made the providential call of my life. I told him about my desire to begin my ministry career in Virginia. He was thrilled because, at the time, there were no evangelical churches in Reston.

As intriguing as that sounded, I had never heard of Reston, which is about 15 miles west of Washington, D.C. It was a very small town at that point, having just been founded in 1964. It started out as a planned community, and the founder was an avowed atheist. He desired to have a community where there would be no crime—a utopia of sorts. Yet within a week of our arrival, there was a murder in the town square. So much for utopia!

Kay and I prayed about it for a week and then phoned Charlie again. It was strange, but we thought, *This must be the*

Lord's call. It seemed divinely appointed. We had a burden to start a work somewhere in Virginia, and now we knew there was a need we could fill. Even though we hadn't met a soul in Reston, we knew Charlie—at least through talking to him on the phone.

So in May of 1974, after I finished two years of Bible college, my wife and I packed up all of our stuff and set sail for Northern Virginia to plant a church in this very unique community. We pulled into Charlie's driveway with $500, no source of income, and no place to live. The Swifts hosted us for a week until we could find an apartment and I could start looking for work. Within the week, both objectives were realized: we had an apartment, and Charlie helped me get an interview for a job at the local country club.

The manager of the country club, Bob, interviewed me for an open position, which would consist of cleaning bathrooms, changing the pool water, and other mundane tasks. But, he said, if I worked at the bar, they would train me to be a bartender and give me an extra $4,000 a year. My initial offer was $6,000 annually, so that was a big jump. (Money was worth a lot more in those days.) I tried to convince myself that since Jesus turned water into wine, a bar gig worth an extra $4,000 would be acceptable. My conscience wasn't buying it. Ultimately, I turned down the bar deal because I didn't think pouring a Bud Light while telling people about the church I was planting would send the right signal. So I accepted the proud title of senior locker room attendant, making $6,000 a year.

Still, I needed to supplement my income. Since the Naval Academy had given me a lot of training in shining shoes, I asked for permission to set up a shoeshine concession for the golfers. The club was fine with that, and they built a little counter for me down near the pro shop. People would drop off their street shoes, which I would clean, while they took their golf cleats out on the course. Then when they brought back their cleats, I'd clean those off and return them to the golfers' lockers.

So there I was, thirty years of age, scrubbing urinals, cleaning pools, and shining shoes, while all of my college buddies had ten years of military or business experience under their belts. I could hardly afford to *buy* a belt. What in the world was I *doing*?

Why hadn't the Lord assigned me to be an assistant pastor at a large church, where I could obtain some practical, hands-on experience? Better yet, why couldn't I have been a candidate for a teaching pastor position at an established church? After all, I did have two years of Bible college under my belt (the belt I could barely afford).

Fortunately, God knew what *he* was doing. My first lesson in ministry was that God often reveals to his children that they can be educated beyond their experience. For example, learning about the strategies and history of warfare and actually stepping into the trenches are two very different worlds. As he did for Gideon's army, the Lord will sometimes subvert everything we think we know to make sure we do not claim any credit or glory for ourselves. So, experience became my teacher and brought me into submission by the providential hand of God, who was preparing me for all that would lie ahead.

The very day I was hired, Bob, the manager, moseyed out from his office while I was laying mulch in front of the club. Since he assumed that I didn't plan to do landscaping for the rest of my life, he started asking me questions about my life and future plans. I told him that I was here to start a church. He looked a bit taken aback and responded by telling me that he was an atheist. As Jesus said, "the harvest is plentiful" (Matt. 9:37), and I was beginning to see the field.

On a hot June evening in 1974, after we had been in Reston about a month, the Swifts opened up their home to be used for a Bible study. It was a thrilling event because I knew that my future congregation would likely include who I met at the country club.

Naturally, I invited Bob to the first Bible study, along with several others from the club. The Swifts asked a few people to come as well. But as the clock struck 7:00 p.m., when the study was supposed to start, Charlie and I were looking at an empty house.

I walked out behind the Swifts' home and stood on the 12th hole of the Reston Country Club, staring at the setting sun and pleading with the Lord to bring people to the study. Suddenly, Bob pulled up in his station wagon. I was ecstatic! It was a bumpy start, but it was a start, nonetheless.

My immediate boss, John, had also been invited, but he hadn't shown up. Charlie, being Charlie, picked up the phone and gave John a subtle reminder. "Hey John, it's casual. Bob is here, and we look forward to seeing you and Terry in a few minutes." Then he quickly hung up. Presumably out of obligation, John and his wife pulled into the driveway minutes later.

So that first study consisted of Bob the atheist manager, John the athletic director and his wife Terry, Kay and me, Charlie and his wife, and another couple they invited. I spoke on the authority of Scripture. It was a very basic apologetic message but certainly one that most of those in the room had never heard.

As an aside, I quickly learned that when you invite people to a Bible study and they say, "I'll try to make it," that is code for, "I absolutely will not be there." I learned this from Harry the golf pro, whom I invited week after week who always "tried" but failed to make it. So one morning in the pro shop I said, "Harry, the study is tonight, and all I ask is that you come one time. If you don't like it, I will never ask you again. I will not ask you to read the Bible out loud or have you pray. Just come and listen to me teach for thirty minutes, have some snacks, and go home." He came. And he never missed another study. Sometimes it just takes removing a few obstacles before people will accept an invite.

Gradually, more and more people would come to the study each week, and I began to identify a trend in this highly intellectual community. There was a prevalent mindset that through education, technology, and scientific pursuit, man would eventually usher in a utopian society. However, the people's lives did not bear witness to that hope. I began to observe the pain that permeated their days as they strived to incorporate human wisdom in order to solve their problems.

The study soon developed into a weekly watering trough where highly educated people came to drink up the truth from a shoeshine boy. My ministry thus became an effort to explain the differences between how the world views life and how God views it. By God's grace and kindness, eyes began to be enlightened, marriages were healed, eternal priorities were set, and the ministry that God called me to was now underway.

Believe it or not, Bob became my very first convert in Virginia. And in God's sovereignty, it was at the country club where I first met the core of my future congregation; this included golf pros, lifeguards, club members, the head chef, the athletic director, and my shoeshine partner.

None of them were believers when I arrived. But through God's handiwork, one of them eventually came on staff at the church, my shoeshine buddy became a missionary to Thailand, and one of the lifeguards married a youth pastor. But the Lord wasn't done yet. After saying "no" to our Bible study for so long, Harry eventually became an elder. Another golf pro became the father of two daughters serving with Campus Crusade, while another ended up leading our missions program for decades, directing millions upon millions of dollars to those spreading the gospel around the world. Still another, who was the child of a club member, came to know Christ and served as our youth pastor for more than thirty years.

My excitement was growing, and the country club became my "fishing" hole. I had such a passion to share the gospel that

I made arrangements to have lunch with different staff members of the club each day. At lunch, I would drive the narrative until we were talking about spiritual matters. The conversations would usually go something like this:

"So tell me, George, do you and your family attend a local church?"

"Sure, we go to the First Bapterian Episcolopian Church of the United Brethren a couple times a year."

"Really? I would be curious to know whether you have the assurance of spending eternity with God?"

"I'm pretty sure I will. After all, I go to church and have lived a good life."

"It's very good to know you have lived a good life! But the question that looms in my mind is: How good do you have to be?"

From there, we were off to the races.

Looking back, those were among the most exciting days of my life. Though I had failed in multiple arenas of life, there was a deep inner conviction that God would build his church and that he would use me in a way that was beyond my wildest imagination or my talents. This was a huge undertaking for a guy like myself whose résumé was held together with duct tape. I have often reminded the people in my church that "God chose the foolish things of the world to shame the wise" (1 Cor. 1:27). I was Exhibit A.

Things went on like this for about a year. I would work at the country club during the week, meeting folks, shining their shoes, and inviting them to come hear about the Bible on Tuesday evenings at the Swifts' house. By that point, there were twenty or twenty-five people coming to the study each week. And those who had been attending for any amount of time knew of my desire to start a church in Reston. One day, Bob confronted me and said, "I'm tired of you talking about how you're going to start a church. Let's start one. As a matter of fact, I've already called the Sheraton Hotel to reserve the meeting space. We are starting in two weeks."

Now I was nervous. I thought, *You mean I'm really going to do this?* I had been hoping I could just talk about it for years and not actually do it. But it seemed the Lord and his servant Bob were not going to let me get away with that. So, in March of 1975, we had the first official meeting of Reston Bible Church in Room G of the Sheraton Hotel. Kay led everyone in singing "Amazing Grace," and I preached from John 3:16.

It was incredible to actually have this thing off the ground, but the church couldn't pay me anything yet. So I would preach a message on Sunday morning in my suit and tie and, then, rush over to the club and slip into my jeans and T-shirt and take my position at the shoeshine booth. As you can imagine, Sunday was a busy day for golfers, and the shoes were coming and going so fast that I could hardly keep up. The people from RBC—the people I had been evangelizing—would come to play golf after church. They would often drop off their shoes and say, "Hey, I really enjoyed the message today, Mike!" Then they'd drop a quarter in my hand. Were they tipping me for the shoes—or the sermon? If it was for the sermon, then I was not off to a great start.

The church started growing rapidly. There just weren't any other churches in the town, and people were telling each other, "You've got to come hear this guy. He's talking about *the Bible!*" So they came, eager to understand the Scriptures and figure out *if* or *how* it could apply to their lives. Because it was all so new to many of them, I did a lot of apologetic teaching in those early days, explaining what the Bible is and why we know it is true.

I knew that all of this had to be God's hand at work because I simply did not possess the inherent leadership and visionary skills this kind of calling should require. Reston is a community that boasts of highly educated people. Many work for the government, military, or big business. We're talking PhD City. What on earth was *I* doing in such a place, and why in the world would a guy with a doctorate listen to a guy like me, whose first college report card was a 0.56? That could only happen in the Lord's upside-down kingdom.

As exciting as it was to see how the Lord was blessing the ministry, I soon became painfully overwhelmed. It reminded me of my plebe year at the Academy. The church was growing faster than I could have imagined, but I didn't know what to do with all these people. Counseling, making hospital visits, preparing for messages, discipling new believers, and evangelizing the lost took up immense amounts of time each week. I had no staff and very few mature believers to lean on. This meant that I was doing all the teaching for a midweek Bible study, a Sunday school class, a Sunday morning service, and an evening service with a limited knowledge of the Word.

I was not drowning—I had already drowned, and I knew it. I had literally taught these people everything I knew about the Scriptures. What was I going to do now? I became so desperate that I looked up old Bible college notes on systematic theology and taught those on Sundays.

While lying in bed one Saturday evening, I told my wife, "I have nothing else to teach. The well has dried up. I need to quit and start looking for a sustainable job." Somehow I got up early that next morning and found something to say from the pulpit, but I knew I couldn't keep drawing from that empty well every week.

A few days later, I called a pastor in a nearby town and asked for help. We met for lunch and I told him my dilemma. I asked him how he could possibly find things to preach week after week, year after year. He suggested that I step away from topical preaching and start doing expository preaching. "That sounds great!" I replied. "What is expository preaching?" He must have been thinking, *Lord, have mercy on this boy.*

He told me to pick a book of the Bible and just teach a few verses each week. *Well, that's a novel idea,* I thought. I had never heard of that before. If my memory serves me correctly, I picked 2 Thessalonians and started teaching through it verse by verse. This new approach was a lifesaver—and a ministry-saver. But it wasn't long before I developed a very strange habit: I studied and meditated for many hours throughout the week, but I did not put my message together until Sunday morning. That is certainly not how I planned to operate, but the sermons just never seemed to come together in my mind before 7:00

a.m. on Sunday mornings. Keep in mind, there was no internet at that time. I could not gather thoughts from other pastors and scholars. And my library was very limited, so I always felt a growing panic as Sunday morning grew closer. But then, just in time, I would get what I call my "Sunday download."

Nothing has changed over the years. When pastors ask me about my preparation routine, I hesitate to tell them, lest they go into cardiac arrest. I don't pretend that this is a good way to prepare for preaching, and I have not recommended it to anyone else. Yet I am so familiar with it by now that I doubt it will ever change.

One Sunday morning I was sitting next to a dear friend who served on the church staff. He leaned over and asked what my message was about so he could pray. I told him I didn't know and needed his prayers to be answered quickly. He said, "I hope you know before you walk up to the pulpit because we are on the final song." I don't remember what I preached on that day, but after that I became known as the "king of wing." You do not necessarily want that on your résumé.

On to North Shore

From there, God took our growing congregation from the Sheraton to the fourth floor of the International Center to the underground classrooms of Terraset Elementary, and then to South Lakes High School. By God's grace, the church continued to outgrow our meeting space, and we finally began to work on a dedicated facility on North Shore Drive in the early 1980s. Yet that building almost didn't make it off the ground.

With the help of a very generous brother named Ralph, we raised enough money to begin working on the new facility. Ralph was so generous that he also volunteered to serve as general contractor for the project, even though he had recently retired as an electrical contractor. His wife, Ruth, had also been diagnosed with cancer, and the outlook was not good. Like many others, Ralph and Ruth had come to know Christ through the witness of one of our members.

Ralph hired all the vendors, from electrical to plumbing to bricklayers. I happily put my John Hancock on all the contracts, and we were ready to go. The mammoth dirt-moving machinery was in place and eager to begin dining on Virginia's red clay. One morning, while noisy engines were waking up a sleepy suburban neighborhood, I was at the hospital visiting a man dying of cancer. The phone in his room rang, and the nurse answered and said it was for me. A bit startled, I grabbed the receiver and said "Hello?" It was my wife Kay. Why would she call me at the hospital? Was everything okay? She quickly informed me that I needed to return home. Ralph had walked off the job! I was stunned, to say the least. How could this be? I had my name on all the contracts. There was no possible way to do this job without a general contractor, and Ralph was doing the work *pro bono*.

Now, I have an innate ability to imagine the worst possible outcome of any situation, particularly in a crisis. As I raced to the elevators, I saw myself in a striped suit with a number stapled under the lapel. I don't even know if lapels are standard attire for convicts, but my extremely imaginative mind had already fast-forwarded to my sentencing. Guilty as charged.

What was the reasoning for his exit? It turned out that one of our elders wrote a note to Ralph, suggesting he stay out of elder business and focus on the building. This did not go over well with a man who had come out of retirement, with a wife dying of cancer, to help a fledgling church build its first sanctuary.

Ralph had left the jobsite and gone to his lake house to distill his emotions and collect himself. I told Kay, "My goose is cooked and we haven't even put it in the oven." My ministry had tanked. What would our testimony be to the neighbors as bright yellow bulldozers sat there dormant? Would this make it into the *Reston Times*? "BIBLE CHURCH RENEGES ON CONTRACT, LEAVING WORKERS WITHOUT PAY."

I continued to run through dire scenarios in my mind. My wife, however, was calm and intuitive. "Mike, you know that Ruth is the love of Ralph's life." That was certainly true, and she had sacrificially given him the green light to pursue this time-consuming project. "Go over and talk to Ruth," Kay said, "and see if things can be cleared up."

I bolted out the front door and nervously drove to Ralph and Ruth's beautiful home. Would she forgive us for the letter? What if she doesn't? My goose may not be in the oven just yet, but it felt like it was on the counter next to it!

I pulled into the driveway and exited my car, which itself was an eyesore in a neighborhood like theirs. I could just hear the gossip. "Who does Ruth know who drives a car like that? Have they lowered their standards?" I knocked on the door and was greeted by Ruth, who pointed the way to the room where we would discuss the matter of the building project, which was also my future. There was no small talk about the weather or how nice the lawns looked at this time of year. We got right down to business.

Here is what Ruth said to me, and I remember it like it was ten minutes ago: "Mike, you didn't write this letter, did you?" (It was signed *Elders of RBC*.) I shook my head. She asked why it was sent, and whether the elders all agreed. I told her it was from *one* elder, and I tried to smooth things over by assuming that he was not thinking clearly and wrote it in haste. Then, I looked Ruth in the eyes and said, "As the lead pastor, I take full responsibility and ask your forgiveness for the hurt this has caused you and Ralph."

She stared back and said, "You are forgiven."

That was music to my ears—but the next words out of her mouth were a symphony to my soul. "I'll have Ralph back on the job first thing in the morning." After my heart regained its rhythm, I thanked her profusely.

Ralph and I agreed to meet on the church property and burn the letter and his prepared letter of resignation. It was the greatest bonfire I have ever been a part of. The heat of forgiveness and reconciliation radiated from two small pieces of paper ignited by the love of Ruth Herring.

I was back at the hospital soon thereafter to visit Ruth. She had started slipping away. Ralph asked me to take her hand and talk to her. Another memory etched in my mind. I reached out and gently grabbed her hand. "Ruth, it's Mike," I said softly. I felt a squeeze and Ralph was so excited. "She heard you. She knows that voice from the pulpit." That made my day. I prayed and soon left the room. As it turned out, she died before I even got to my car. We buried her a few days later. *Bittersweet* is what ministry is all about.

Looking Back

In some respects, real spiritual therapy is taking place as I chronicle God's faithfulness in my life. I say "therapy" because as I am writing, I am coming out of the most painful trial I have experienced over the years. The pressure has seemed unbearable at times, but as I rehearse what God has done over the years, what right do I, as the clay, have to question the potter (Rom. 9:21)? He is fashioning me and conforming me to his image, as he promised he would (Rom. 8:29).

I well remember the time I observed Michelangelo's sculptures in Florence, Italy. Some of his work was unfinished and all I could see was part of a body trying to emerge from its marble prison. As the great sculptor is often thought to have said about creating his masterpiece *David*: "You just chip away the stone that doesn't look like David." In the same vein, if we want to look more like Christ to our people, then God must chip away all that doesn't look like him.

How does the Lord sculpt us to look like Christ? Very often it is through hard times. Pastors are often told to just "hang in there" during seasons of trial, but that implies our only goal is survival. Scripture, however, tells us to "consider it pure joy . . . whenever you face trials of many kinds" (James 1:2). So we must rejoice even in those hard times that seem to grow abundantly in the rocky soil of ministry. We must see Christ leading us through the deep waters and storms of our calling. Difficult as it may be, we must always remember that this is *his* church, not ours, and that, as pastors, we are first and foremost pilgrims leading our people in search of a city "with foundations, whose architect and builder is God" (Heb. 11:10).

Difficulties will come in many forms. If a sterling reputation is your goal, then consider the words of Paul about our Savior: He "made Himself of no reputation, taking the form of a bondservant, and coming in the likeness of men" (Phil. 2:7 NKJV).

If riches are your goal—and let's face it, there is a lot of money being made in the name of Christ these days—then listen to the words of Jesus: "Foxes have dens and birds have nests, but the Son of Man has no place to lay his head" (Matt. 8:20).

If life is your supreme love, then ponder how much Paul longed to die: "For me, to live is Christ and to die is gain" (Phil. 1:21).

If close friends are what you want, then meditate on the following words of King David: "Even my own familiar friend in whom I trusted, who ate my bread, has lifted up his heel against me" (Ps. 41:9 NKJV). Or these from the apostle Paul:

"Demas, because he loved this world, has deserted me and has gone to Thessalonica" (2 Tim. 4:10).

If safety is paramount, then consider these words concerning Moses: "He chose to be mistreated along with the people of God rather than to enjoy the fleeting pleasures of sin" (Heb. 11:25).

If peace is at the top of your list, then think upon these words of Paul to Timothy: "You therefore must endure hardship as a good soldier of Jesus Christ. No one engaged in warfare entangles himself with the affairs of this life, that he may please him who enlisted him as a soldier" (2 Tim. 2:3–4 NKJV).

If glory ranks high on your priority list, make sure it is biblical, pastoral glory. "Therefore I will boast all the more gladly about my weaknesses, so that Christ's power may rest on me" (2 Cor. 12:9).

If power is what you so desire, then you might join the ranks of Simon the Sorcerer who said, "Give me this power also . . ." (Acts 8:19 NKJV). Better to remember where the real power is: "For the message of the cross is foolishness to those who are perishing, but to us who are being saved it is the power of God" (1 Cor. 1:18).

I, for one, would rather live life on the edge with Christ as my guide than wallow in the safety of the mundane, only to realize I made no impact for the kingdom of God. Wouldn't you?

PART 2

CHAPTER 4

A PASTOR'S GUIDE

B efore we go much deeper, I want to talk about you. Pastor, I've just opened up about my life, so now let's talk about you for a bit. I know that, like many pastors, you fear that your flock would feel quite insecure if it were to leak out that you are struggling. You live in fear that people might actually see you as a real person and not as a spiritual Superman. I know how you feel.

I know about the nasty email you received this past week detailing your every failure as a leader. I know how it feels to have no stone left unturned to discover your every flaw.

I know what it was like when you finished your series on "The Victorious Christian Life," only to feel much better acquainted with defeat. Did it make you feel like a hypocrite?

What about the latest grumblings that your preaching lacks depth, or that you are boring, or that you are too old, or that you are too young?

How did it make you feel when some of your closest friends suggested that you go on a sabbatical because you have lost your passion for ministry and the wheels seem to be coming off? Did it make you look inward and say, "How could this be happening to me if I have the Holy Spirit and the power of Christ to strengthen me?" Did you begin to question your calling or your theology? Or both? Be honest with me.

How did it feel when a member of your congregation questioned one of your pet doctrines and you found yourself unable to give an adequate defense? Did you start to question your ability to handle other cherished doctrines of the faith? Did you begin to wonder if you had been adequately trained for this thing we call Christian ministry? This is just between you and me.

Have you ever wondered why you are able to give such great counsel to others who are hurting but can't seem to comfort your own soul?

Maybe you've gone through depression—or maybe you are going through it now. Is it because you are worried about the church finances or the potential split brewing in the body that you don't know how to stop? Is all this going on while you are dealing with a prodigal at home and your wife is wishing that you could find another career, but you realize that you have no training for anything else in life? Are these the anxieties that are plaguing your soul?

I know the loneliness that you feel when there seems to be no one to turn to. After all, a shepherd doesn't ask his sheep for advice, right?

Tell me about the vortex that ministry has created in your life. How do you feel when you are being swallowed up by endless criticism? How does it hit you when you go online and see a young pastor who started a church in his garage four years ago and is now running twenty thousand and is forced to meet in a basketball stadium? Do you feel like you missed the anointing? Are you battling with jealousy?

Having pastored for such a long time at the same church, having traveled extensively, and having talked to hundreds of pastors who have told me their worst ministry nightmares (and having experienced many myself), I feel qualified to help you in this journey. Does this make me an expert? I don't think anyone is an expert in shepherding, but I've had a lot of time behind the ministry wheel. And I hope that what I share will help you stay the course.

I will make two promises up front. First, I promise not to make this a pity party. We will not spend all of our time talking about how hard ministry is. All professions in life have their challenges. Ministry is no exception. There are some very unique challenges in ministry that we must address, but there are also abundant blessings that can only be experienced by those with our calling.

Secondly, we will exalt the Lord Jesus throughout these pages and recognize him as the one who will take us through the fire. We will keep in mind that pastoring is a high calling and must be met with tears of joy. If that appeals to you, then let's get started.

Get ready for a deep dive. I have written this section—this whole book, actually—to give hope to those who find the ministry challenging and discouraging. If you are just starting your journey as a pastor, I trust that these words will help prepare you for the highs and lows that you will soon face. If you are a seasoned veteran, then my prayer is that you would find encouragement to trust the Lord, weather the storms, and stay the course.

Let me also mention that I think the words of this book will have value for you whether you lead an eighty-person congregation in rural Texas or an 8,000-person congregation in downtown New York City. There are unique opportunities, temptations, and challenges that come with any kind of church. As for me, I am somewhat in the middle of the pack—I pastor a megachurch but not a "mega mega" church. It started very small and grew over time, not overnight. If you are pastor of a small or medium-sized church, you might be tempted to feel inadequate compared to our brothers who steward the megachurches and live in the spotlight. But we must ask ourselves: Do we really want the pressure that comes with such a spotlight? Do we want our every sermon critiqued on some blog somewhere? Do we want social media to explode whenever we are misunderstood? Those nationally and internationally known pastors breathe rarified air and, in many cases, probably wish they were shepherding a flock of eighty.

Truth be known, I used to be very introspective about such issues and wrestled with jealousy. I just couldn't seem to find the formula. I often asked myself, *What do these people have that I don't? What's the secret sauce?* We are too often inclined to this kind of thinking, even when we all know the dangers of comparing ourselves to those who have been sovereignly gifted in ways we are not. The Lord has raised up some of you to speak to large congregations, give countless media interviews, or teach at major conferences. He has equipped others of us to minister to smaller crowds. One is not better than the other; they are just different.

Whatever your situation, you have been given a great responsibility that must be maintained with a humble spirit. We all know of pastors and ministry leaders who have raised themselves up for their own glory. Make no mistake; God can weed out the proud. Wherever the Lord has placed you right now, you must see yourself as his servant. "For everyone to whom much is given, from him much will be required" (Luke 12:48 NKJV).

Remember, you are not being graded here, for no one but God in heaven has the right to say, "Well done, good and faithful servant" (Matt. 25:21). From here, we will look at troubling things in the church today that are causing great division. We will assess our individual skill sets and find ways to maximize them. We will explore some great burdens and rejoice in God's amazing grace. My desire is to help you navigate the beautiful but often turbulent waters of ministry. Ours is a unique vocation in every way, and one well worth living out in his strength. So let's get started and see what the Lord has for us.

And for those of you who have picked up this book but are not in pastoral ministry, you are more than welcome to eavesdrop. You may find some truths that will help you as you minister to friends or neighbors, or you may gain new ways to encourage your own pastor. Every pastor needs to know the body is behind him. He gets enough criticism and a little encouragement goes a long way. It will help him to confirm that his calling is truly from the Lord.

CHAPTER 5

THE PASTOR AND HIS CALLING

I can't tell you how many times people have asked me to describe how I was called into ministry. Some want to know how to discern whether they have been given that call. In truth, the call is not complicated. Romans 12 tells us that if you present yourself "as a living sacrifice, holy and pleasing to God" (v. 1) and if you are not conformed to this world, then the Lord will let you know what his will is for you. You will know if you have been called to ministry. In this chapter, we will explore what it means to be called to lead a church and what God expects of his shepherds.

Who Is Sufficient for Such a Task?

We are talking about the calling of ministry, but what exactly have we been called *to*? Does the Bible give us a clear, singular job description, or do we fly by the seat of our pants and make things up as we go along? Do we just imitate Jesus or Paul as examples for how to be good shepherds? Have we made this calling more complex than it should be? Do we put ourselves under unnecessary pressure? How on earth do we fulfill our calling—is there a blueprint to follow?

As I read through the Scriptures, I don't see any clear set of instructions for shepherding. Yes, Paul said to "follow my example, as I follow the example of Christ" (1 Cor. 11:1), but Paul never fed five thousand, walked on water, or was raised from the grave. So, I don't think he means that we are to do *everything* Jesus did. Likewise, when Paul exhorted us to "let this mind be in you which was also in Christ Jesus" (Phil. 2:5 NKJV), he obviously was not expecting us to be omniscient. Having the mind of Christ does not mean we will know all that he knows, but that we will think as he thinks.

God has sovereignly placed you where he wants you. He has given you the people *he* wants *you* to shepherd. I once delivered a message to our body, and a visiting pastor came up to me and said, "Isn't it funny that your message is just perfect for Northern Virginia, but that message would never relate to where I pastor." He was not claiming that truth is relative, by any means. He meant that what his people are starving for, in the way of biblical nourishment, is very different from what my people need. Different areas of the world, and even different areas within your city, have unique challenges, temptations, and social dynamics that affect how they hear the Word. A message about guarding our eyes from sensual imagery would be quite relevant to a society that is saturated with lust-provoking TV shows, but such a warning may not be as urgent in the jungles of New Guinea. The sinful human heart is the same everywhere, but its ability to express its sinfulness is drawn out differently from culture to culture.

So first, it is critical to know the "condition of your flocks" (Prov. 27:23). Study your people. Look for common problems that they all seem to face. For example, materialism would be more pronounced in an American megachurch than in a house church in China. Paul corrected those at Corinth by addressing problems that were inherent to their culture.

Second, remember that even though problems may differ, the solution is always found in Jesus. No matter the culture, social status, environment, and income, all have an effect on what is highlighted in your preaching: Christ is the door to salvation. Paul always appealed to his readers by bringing them face-to-face with the risen Savior. The topic didn't matter. If it was money, Paul said that "though he was rich, yet for your sake he became poor, so that you through his poverty might become rich" (2 Cor. 8:9). If it was immorality, Paul said, "Do you not know that your bodies are members of Christ? Shall I then take the members of Christ and make them members of a harlot? Certainly not!" (1 Cor. 6:15 NKJV). If it was marriage, then Paul admonished husbands to "love your wives, just as

Christ loved the church and gave himself up for her" (Eph. 5:25). If it was forgiveness, he told his readers, "Bear with each other and forgive one another if any of you has a grievance against someone. Forgive as the Lord forgave you" (Col. 3:13). If it was death, then Paul said, "Indeed, we felt that we had received the sentence of death. But that was to make us rely not on ourselves but on God who raises the dead" (2 Cor. 1:9 ESV). If it was life, then he reminded us that Christ "is your life" (Col. 3:4). You get the picture. No matter the subject, Christ must be preached as the ultimate salvation and satisfaction. By knowing and studying your people, you will know how to apply the all-sufficiency of Christ to their situation.

We are called to follow the example of Christ, but we are also called to be an example for others to follow. What exactly does that look like? I know I have never seen anyone who perfectly reflected the character and nature of Christ himself. We are tarnished images, yet by the grace of God we are called to reflect his glory. As I look at those I have admired over the years, some have been known for their great faith, while others were recognized as great servants. Some sacrificed beyond measure, while others preached with great boldness. None of us can possess a character that looks just like Christ, but each of us has something to offer. As shepherds, we must be taking daily inventory of our lives and making all of the necessary mid-course corrections. We live life on purpose. "I press toward the mark for the prize of the high calling of God in Christ Jesus" (Phil. 3:14 KJV). This is our great and glorious mission.

Being an example worth following does not require a mystical way of living, nor does it mean you will be performing miracles. Rather, it is a call to live an uncomplicated life that is not entangled "with the affairs of this life" (2 Tim. 2:4 NKJV). Note that Paul wrote those words to a young pastor, Timothy, who was no doubt tempted in many of the same ways we are.

So be an example to your flock, Pastor. Live in such a way that people want to emulate your faith and character. When our flock sees that we are just "sojourners and pilgrims" (1 Pet. 2:11 NKJV) passing through this world and that our lives reflect this eternal perspective, they will be encouraged to follow. If we, like Abraham, are "looking forward to the city with foundations, whose architect and builder is God" (Heb. 11:10), our people will start looking for that same city. Teach your people to live with eternity in mind. Stretch their faith with messages that challenge them beyond their human limits by appealing to their understanding of Christ living his life through them. "How to" messages that don't point to Christ as our help and Savior are just appeals to the flesh to try a little harder.

Finally, Pastor, as you strive to serve your congregation, don't forget to shepherd those closest to you—your family. Fall in love with your wife and children over and over again. This must be paramount. Failing to lead those under your roof is no small failure. I am not suggesting that you won't have a prodigal child. God may assign you such a trial, but your love must never waver during those hard times. Keep the fatted calf in the barn, for you never know when you will be called upon to slay it (Luke 15:23). Your family must never be more precious than Christ, but your love for them should reflect the love of Christ. Your family is church in miniature form. They must be cared for above all else. We will talk more about this vital ministry in the next chapter.

Stay in Your Sandbox

I enter this next arena cautiously, but it is important. Each of us has differing habits, giftings, experience, and education. I have already discussed my own strange thinking habits, cognitive delay, and minimal formal training. With that in mind, we pastors must learn to play in our own "sandboxes." God has created you in a specific way for a specific purpose, to pastor a certain congregation in a certain location. Your strategy cannot be simply to copy another pastor you admire. He may be wired differently than you or live in a completely different context. They are who they are and you are who you are, "by the grace of God" (1 Cor. 15:10).

Here is an illustration of what I mean by staying in your own sandbox: Suppose you are tone deaf but desire to be a great singer. You could hire the best vocal coach in the world, but your improvement (or lack thereof) will not be based on his or her ability to coach you but on the limitations of your natural giftedness. In other words, you will be limited because your ability is limited.

This leads me into the pastor's study. We are all very different and need to stay within the limits God has given us. I love talking to different pastors and find out how they prepare for messages. I can learn and gain helpful hints that may supplement my present study habits, but I also realize that the way God has made me is so different from that of others. As you've already discovered, I probably have one of the most radical message preparation strategies of any pastor on the planet. Therefore, I never encourage anyone to do what I do—meditating on a Scripture text all week and waiting until Saturday or Sunday for a message "download." I wouldn't wish that on anyone, but it's part of my sandbox. You might say, "Why don't you discipline yourself to have it done earlier?" I have tried, but nothing seems to come until about two hours before I preach.

Some of you are the opposite. You may be very gifted at outlining your sermons. You put things together in a very logical way—it's how God made you. I am a meditator, and this is how God speaks to me. I am also gifted in being able to speak off-the-cuff. That comes easy to me. I personally feel awkward looking down at notes, yet I have seen men deliver brilliant sermons from well-organized notes. We are all different.

Since I have no seminary training myself, I will often tap into some scholarly work or commentary to see if there is something I am missing. I read what others have said about the text I plan to teach on, but that is not where I derive my main thoughts. Interestingly enough, what I have often found is that the scholars, through meditation, have discovered many insights that are not a result of their scholarship. This should give hope to those of us who are lacking a Master of Divinity degree. I am reminded of the men on the road to Emmaus who said to one another, "Were not our hearts burning within us while he talked with us on the road and opened the Scriptures to us?" (Luke 24:32).

Christ is always the ultimate teacher. Scholarship is beneficial, but it is not the final authority. Illumination from the Spirit of Christ is the key factor. Later on in the same chapter of Luke, it says that the Lord "opened their minds so they could understand the Scriptures" (Luke 24:45). Those disciples walking with Jesus were ordinary men with no formal training.

Sticking to your own sandbox will also help you resist the urge to borrow a message from another pastor you like to listen to. And by "borrow" I mean "plagiarize." I understand the temptation, but to preach what is not yours will never come from the heart and will lead your people to believe that you spent hours preparing a sermon you didn't create. That is an intent to deceive and is not honoring to God. Yes, we all lean on other sources here and there, but to repackage a whole message falls into another category. Whenever I dip into another source with a really juicy insight, I always give credit to the source. (Our congregation knows I'm not that sharp anyway!) As the late Warren Wiersbe used to say, "I milk a lot of cows, but I make my own butter."

Your style of speaking and preaching is another area where you may be inclined to emulate a well-known pastor, but your flock will be served better if you embrace how God has wired you. Some preachers are very passionate and raise their voice to drive home a point. I have seen others try to force themselves to do the same thing, and it looks very strange and out of place.

Everyone is uncomfortable. To go back to our earlier example, it is like someone who thinks they can sing but cannot carry a tune. The audience will end up looking at the floor in embarrassment. Your natural preaching style may be dramatic and commanding or soft-spoken and gentle. Either way, you will be most effective when you stay in your sandbox. I know it is popular advice to "get out of your comfort zone," but in this case, I encourage you to lean *into* your comfort zone as though it were a trusted friend. Your congregation will be all the more blessed for it.

Faithfulness, Not Results

How well I remember my first mission trip into the deepest jungles of Bolivia. Five families were stationed along a river in an effort to contact a nomadic tribe that had not yet heard the promises of Christ. When I arrived, the team leader asked if I would give devotions the following evening. *Piece of cake,* I thought, since I had plenty of sermons in my back pocket, ready to be pulled out at a moment's notice. *Preparation won't even be necessary.*

I could give one of my favorite messages on the dangers of loving the world. *Oh, that's right, there are no malls down here.*

No problem. I could talk about the importance of commitment. *Commitment? To a group of people who have given up everything for the sake of the gospel?*

The more I thought about my messages, the sooner I realized that they had all been delivered in the comfortable and sterile environment of Northern Virginia. In my Sunday morning teaching, I often had to warn against the dangers of prosperity, the allure of the corporate ladder, or the pitfalls of power. But what could I say to a group of people who had sacrificed their comfort and security to see the kingdom advanced?

I began to panic, but the Lord soon led me to 1 Corinthians 4:2: "Moreover it is required in stewards, that a man be found faithful" (NKJV). I was able to minister to their discouraged hearts and remind them that results might take years to see, not weeks. As Hebrews 11:13 says of the saints of old: "These all died in faith, not having received the promises, but having seen them afar off, were assured of them, embraced them, and confessed that they were strangers and pilgrims on the earth" (NKJV).

God is not interested in our results, but in our faithfulness. Maybe you minister in a concrete jungle instead of one that is waterlogged and snake-infested, but it is a jungle, nonetheless, overgrown with sin and full of people needing a way out. So how do you handle it when your efforts seem to be failing and "there are no grapes on the vines" of your ministry (Hab. 3:17)? What will keep you going?

Working in the Lord's vineyard is often difficult and discouraging. Not every pastor will experience the growth of a megachurch. Vineyards come in all shapes and sizes, and the Lord knows exactly what you need to fulfill what he has called you to. At this point, you hopefully know something about my abilities, gifts, talents, and weaknesses so you can better understand me and relate in a more effective way to what I'm sharing.

I remember once hearing Saddleback pastor Rick Warren speak to a group of pastors in a nationwide simulcast. In his warm and engaging fashion, Rick said, "If I can do it, anyone can!" Though I appreciate his self-effacing manner, I wanted to stand up and shout, "No, Rick, we can't!" Men like Rick Warren are ten-talent guys who could run General Motors during a coffee break. I believe he meant what he said, but people who fly at higher altitudes are often deprived of the oxygen of reality and thus make dizzying statements to us mortals who live at sea level. I have also been to John MacArthur's Shepherds' Conference. I will never be able to exegete a text to the degree and with the precision he can. God has given John MacArthur and Rick Warren the unique grace to lead their churches—and he has done the same for you and me.

As for myself, I don't have a take-charge personality. I'm not constantly looking for the next hill to climb. But that does not mean I have never been tempted to leave my sandbox. One day several years ago, I woke up to the realization that I had exchanged my rod and staff for a cell phone and computer. I was operating more like the president and CEO of a large organization than the pastor of a local church. The flock I was shepherding had morphed into a corporate enterprise, and the search for biblical truth was eclipsed by questions like, "Where are we headed as an organization? Do we have a mission statement? What are our long-range goals?"

Such questions were completely foreign to my thinking. I am not a goal setter, vision caster, core-value promoter, or mission statement writer. That's just not me. I can barely think past lunch, much less draw up a five-year plan. I am not suggesting those things are wrong in and of themselves, but it does concern me that for every seminar on prayer or holiness, it seems like there are a hundred on leadership. This paradigm shift from shepherd to "leader" is huge, and few pastors know how to handle it.

People are so accustomed to powerful leaders in the world that they look for the same characteristics in their pastors. But what if, by nature, you aren't a "gifted leader" as the world defines it? This is exactly where I find myself. I have faithfully taught the Scriptures, and, by God's grace, the church has grown through the years to where it eventually averaged 2,400 in weekly attendance with four weekend services. I realize that may not be as large as many of today's megachurches, but it is bigger than most. All of a sudden, I found myself as a corporate executive running a multi-million-dollar organization with no ability or giftedness to keep this thing we call "church" going. That's not something I ever could have imagined when I gave my first sermon to twenty-five people in a hotel meeting room in 1975. I found the leadership responsibilities crushing. Many people asked me, "Where are we going as a church?" My response was always the same: "I didn't know we were on a trip!"

Since faithfulness, and not results, is what God asks of us, we can be assured that his "power is made perfect in weakness"

(2 Cor. 12:9), and we can lead confidently with the skills he has lovingly provided to us.

Do I Stay or Do I Go?

When I came to Reston to plant a church, my wife and I lived in a low-income housing project where nights were often filled with wailing police sirens and drug raids. I generally couldn't sleep, which was particularly bad on Saturdays when I had to preach the next morning. I remember one Saturday night that was particularly bad, and I yelled out to God (okay, more like yelled *at* God) to let him know that I was doing *him* a favor by planting a church for *him* and that the least *he* could do would be to keep the racket down outside my window so I could preach in the morning. Obviously, the truth is that God was doing *me* the favor to even allow me to be on his team.

I think every pastor must occasionally take a good, hard look at his calling to see whether he is feeling sorry for himself. We are called to war, and war is never easy. There is a lot of hurt along the way. God called Paul to spread the gospel but also show him "how much he must suffer for my name" (Acts 9:16). Admittedly, Paul was an apostle with a unique calling, but it is safe to say that we pastors are also called to expect hardship.

Is there ever a time to step away from the ministry or even to realize that the pastoral ministry was never actually your calling? This is a big question and one that I think needs to be addressed with some honest reflection. Are you falling out of love for your people? Do you feel the grace of God is no longer sustaining you? Have you lost interest in ministry? Did you get into ministry for the wrong reasons?

I once ordained a young man who really wanted to plant a church. I admit that I was not sure this was his calling from God. He simply didn't have the heart of a pastor. But I sent him out with my blessing. It soon became obvious, however, that the fruit of his labor was divisiveness, and the people he angered justifiably blamed me. He is no longer in the ministry and rightly so.

To be clear, just because you answer "yes" to one of the above questions—or all of them—doesn't automatically mean it is time to jump ship. There have been multiple times when I have come close to throwing in the towel, but in the nick of time, God's grace rescued me. His power showed up, and it became obvious that he was not finished with me. When he is ready for me to move on, he will make sure that I am the first one to know (or perhaps second to my wife or those closest to me).

There were plenty of men in Scripture who felt God had hung them out to dry. Not the least of these was Moses, who wanted to die when the burden of leading a grumbling people became too much. "If this is how you are going to treat me, please go ahead and kill me—if I have found favor in your eyes—and do not let me face my own ruin" (Num. 11:15). But the Lord was not finished with him. There was much work to be done, and God's grace and power provided the way.

So we must be careful in our self-analysis to avoid the following pitfalls:

> **Pitfall 1:** Premature action. Sometimes we want out because the going has gotten really tough and we can't see light at the end of the tunnel. Yet, as we'll see later in this book, God blesses those who endure.

> **Pitfall 2:** Rationalization. We begin to say things like, "With all that I do for God, if this is how I get treated, then I am out of here!" This kind of attitude comes from sinful pride. If the apostles—not to mention our Lord himself—suffered so much in their ministries, why should we be different?

If you are still beginning to feel like it might be time to hang it up, here are a few more questions you should ask yourself:

1. Have you given your ministry enough time to develop?
2. Are numbers (attendance, conversions, baptisms), or the lack thereof, the primary factor shaping your decision?
3. Do you perhaps just need a break and some time to get away and get recharged?

4. Are you fighting a battle that you think you need to win because "failure" is not in your vocabulary?

5. Are you staying in the fight out of personal pride or for the glory of God?

6. Is there a competitive spirit that keeps you pressing on while your wife and children are unduly suffering?

These are tough questions, but you serve no one if you don't have the call to ministry and stay anyway. Nor are you doing anyone a favor if you quit when God has truly called you. Either way, make sure you are not working through this alone. I have had plenty of men in my life who have encouraged me when things got tough. Make certain your leadership team knows of your struggles. Getting a different perspective will be of enormous help. Older saints, who have walked in your shoes years before you walked in them, can give wise counsel that will help you stay the course. Pray as you have never prayed before.

CHAPTER 6

THE PASTOR AND HIS FAMILY

S hepherding your family is one of the most wonderful and difficult challenges you will ever encounter. The enemy knows our vulnerabilities and will take every advantage to secure a beachhead. The devil knows that if he can dismantle the pastor's family, he can also dismantle the church. But if a pastor leads his home well, his ministry will be all the better for it.

Easing the Pressure

As a pastor or ministry leader, we are called to have lives that are above reproach. Thus, our marriages are to be pristine and our children are always paragons of virtue, right? Such self-imposed standards will exacerbate any struggles within the family. Smiles pasted on the children and a wife living under the pressure of her husband's demand that she be cheerful at all times lest people think there is a problem, will only quench the Spirit. Your family should be themselves. Will some people have unrealistic expectations? Yes, but my experience has been that most won't. As pastors, when we hear a complaint about our wife or children, we tend to assume that everyone must be in agreement with the complaint. This is natural, but far from reality. When my daughter Kelly was attending a Christian school, a teacher once accused her of lying. "Pastor's kids should never lie," she said. Kelly immediately thought, *Is it okay for a carpenter's kid to lie?*

When Reston Bible Church was about a year old, I stood before the body and said, "Today's sermon is going to be on the role of the pastor and his wife." Now there's a message that will get your people's attention! I spoke for about forty minutes on my role as a shepherd. I then said, "Now let me tell you about my wife's role. She has the same calling as any other woman in the church. There is no biblical job description for a pastor's wife. She is to shepherd our children and guide our home. She will not be involved in every ministry in the church but will serve where she is gifted." That part of the message took about one minute. They got the point.

You can't keep people from watching your family, but you can find ways to ease some of the pressure. If your children are still young, sit them down and tell them that you desire to see them behave in a godly fashion, but you do not want them to feel that they can't be themselves.

My youth pastor and his wife have nine children and have been with our church for more than thirty-three years. Can you imagine the pressure of being a youth pastor who is helping the rest of us raise our kids, while at the same time trying to show us what success looks like by raising nine of your own?

Yes, we do have bull's-eyes painted on our chests. Yes, some people will take target practice on our family, but if the truth were known, most people will look at us and say, "I could never do what you do." Most people will cut you a break and have some sense of what it must be like to be a pastor's kid or a pastor's wife. There is probably much more admiration than judgment. We, however, have the tendency to take the seeds of condemnation and plant them in our minds. We water and fertilize them with wild imaginations, and before long, we convince ourselves that everyone despises us.

Most young men in ministry have visions of raising perfect children. After all, we know what the Bible teaches and may be convinced that the application of biblical truths will guarantee model offspring. Reality strikes soon after the birth of your first child. You begin to see that Adam's sinful nature is alive and well. Strong-willed tendencies will show up, and you feel like you should get this under control because everyone is watching—and you're supposed to be the expert. The teen years hit and you trade in bibs for boxing gloves as you find that your children have the same normal tendencies to love the world as do other children. Somehow coming through a pastoral line doesn't exempt them from struggling with the sin from within. You might fear embarrassment if they do not follow in your theological footsteps. You may begin to worry about job security. Doesn't the Bible tell us that we must have children who "believe and are not open to the charge of being wild and disobedient" (Titus 1:6)? Doesn't Proverbs tell us that if we "train up a child in the way he should go, and when he is old, he will not depart from it" (Prov. 22:6 NKJV)?

Yes, but here is something to keep in mind: You are not responsible for how your children turn out, but you are responsible to "bring them up in the training and instruction of the Lord" (Eph. 6:4). They are morally obligated to take it from there. The family is the foundation of society, and certainly every pastor and his wife should do everything in their power to live a life free of hypocrisy before their children. They must be able to observe that what you profess from the pulpit and at home are free from pretense. This is where they see the Christian life lived out—not in theory but in reality.

I made plenty of serious mistakes while raising my four kids. All of them have turned out well, but only by God's grace. One of the things we did each year was to be sure to take a family vacation. There were times in the early days when we had to scrape our pennies together, but it was worth it. Taking hikes, fishing, and swimming in the ocean secured happy memories for a lifetime. When we all get together, we reminisce and laugh hysterically. These are healthy memories that rejuvenate the soul.

This might surprise you, but we never had family devotions. Never! Well, that is not true. We had them once, and that is why we never had them again. It was a disaster, and I didn't want the kids growing up hating the Bible. That is certainly not to say family devotions are bad. I just wasn't good at it and found other ways to slip the spinach into the ice cream. Deuteronomy 6 talks about teaching your children throughout the day. We are to use *every* opportunity to instruct them about the ways of the world and the ways of God.

They will see the word in action and not just at a designated family time. For instance, I might walk through the woods and point out the complexity of a spider web and ask them, "Do you believe this just happened by chance?" Then we could talk about God's creative power.

A final thought: When you, as a parent, offend your children, never think, "I'm the parent, and I don't need to seek forgiveness." That is a mortal flaw. When you have been wrong, but sweep it under the carpet out of pride, you have done a great disservice to your children. They have long memories. The carpet will eventually become a mountain that separates you from your offspring. They will clearly remember and may hold a grudge all the way to the grave. Deal with it now.

The Great Battle

Before we leave this discussion on the family, I must address what I believe is one of the greatest threats to your family, to our nation, and to the world—and that is pornography. I came out of a military home, and I know that great threats exist that will kill the body, but this one will kill the soul.

Pastor, lust is a temptation that we all battle. When I was in my forties, I thought, *When I get to be fifty, this battle won't be as hard.* When I was in my fifties, I thought, *I'm sure it's going to die down soon.* Well, I'm in my late seventies and the battle is just as hard as when I was seventeen. It doesn't go away.

By God's grace, I am not hooked on pornography. If I was, I'd go before the elders and resign. But that doesn't mean I don't have temptations and struggles. I know that this battle is raging and so, so strong. Listen, Pastor: if left unguarded, this temptation will take you down. It will take you out of the game and destroy your ministry. It doesn't mean you're going to lose your salvation, but it is a battle that you must fight diligently. So how can we win?

The first step is to be clear that your identity is in Christ alone. Galatians 2:20 says, "I have been crucified with Christ and I no longer live, but Christ lives in me. The life I now live in the body, I live by faith in the Son of God, who loved me and gave himself for me."

We have been crucified with Christ. Crucifixion is death. When Jesus died, I died. So your identity in Christ has to do with the fact that he is the one who is living his life through you. You cannot live the Christian life; only Christ can live the Christian life. Having died with Christ, we are now "slaves to righteousness" (Rom. 6:18), and "we should no longer be slaves to sin" (Rom. 6:6).

You may feel that you are a slave to your flesh, but we have to believe what God says is true of our new identity. We died with Christ, and he lives in us. That is not easy to grasp, and it is a lifelong understanding of who we are. But what the Scripture is telling us is that *we cannot fight this battle*, or any other battle, for that matter, unless Christ is the one doing the fighting.

Believe that the Savior is fighting for you, and treasure him above all else. That doesn't mean that temptation will lose its sting or bite. It will still be there, but it starts to pale in comparison to the beauty of the Lord. You will find that when the temptation comes—and it is always just a click away—you realize that your heavenly Father is far more important and you identify with his Son. The more that sinks deep within your soul and the more of a reality that becomes, the more victory you have in this battle.

But don't just stop there. You also must be careful not to put yourself in a position to fall. That's not easy, either. Paul told Timothy to "flee also youthful lusts" (2 Tim. 2:22 NKJV), but I sometimes want to ask the Lord: *Where would I flee?* You need to have a phone and you need to have a computer to operate in this world. That means you must be vigilant. Today you can visit the "house" of the seductress (Prov. 5:8) without ever leaving yours. One of the ways I protect myself is not having a TV in my bedroom. There is too much temptation to flip through the channels and see something that would stir up lustful thoughts. I don't judge others for having a TV there, but I just can't have that temptation lurking when I am getting ready for bed. Psalm 101:3 says, "I will not look with approval on anything that is vile." How much of our entertainment would we need to remove if we took this seriously? "Rather, clothe yourselves with the Lord Jesus Christ, and do not think about how to gratify the desires of the flesh" (Rom. 13:14).

So meditate on Scripture that points to your identity in Christ. Put those things aside that would pull you away from treasuring him. And be prepared to shepherd your children and your church through their own battles.

CHAPTER 7

THE PASTOR
AND PRIDE

Pastor, there is a terrifying monster that each of us is going to face. It will find you when you're preaching. It will appear when you prepare a message. It will pursue you when you are counseling, and it will track you down in church staff meetings. It will tell you how amazing you are—as such a brilliant orator, no wonder so many people came to hear you preach! It will try to set up a dwelling in your very soul, and it will not be easily evicted.

This monster's name is *pride*.

Pride in the Pulpit

No matter who you are or how long you've been in ministry, you won't conquer this denizen of the deep. It is a most determined foe. After all my decades of preaching, I still find myself constantly under pride's assault. Even as I write this book, I wonder how high it will end up on the *New York Times* Best Sellers List. (Very high, I am sure.)

When pride first appeared on the scene, it began its attack in the form of a simple question, offered to an audience of one: "Did God really say . . . ?" (Gen. 3:1). Those words have echoed down the corridors of human history and still lead people astray to this day. And pride saves some of its most vicious attacks for when we are in the pulpit. After all, that's when pastors are most eager to shine. Pride would have us worry more about performing than preaching. It is a fine line, but true preaching comes under the leadership of the Holy Spirit and always manifests humility. A performance, on the other hand, brings with it a prideful desire to rob God of his glory and transfer it to ourselves.

Pride escorts us to the stage and reassures us that the power of our gifted presence is enough to change the hearts of people. (If not, it is *their* fault for not listening well enough.) Pride whispers to us that God is lucky to have us, along with all our talent, teaching his people. Pride encourages us to view ministry as a competition, where we must strive to have the greatest market share of souls saved, outdoing all the other churches around. In all this, this crafty enemy deceives us into thinking that we are *actually* quite humble, given all of the amazing things we do for the kingdom.

Pride reminds us of our expansive biblical knowledge and how deftly we can decimate anyone who dares question our doctrine. Pride tells us that being right is of utmost importance—otherwise, we might look bad! Pride encourages us to wallow in self-pity and shift the blame of any church problems to everywhere except the pulpit. It nudges us to rely on logic more than Scripture because, pride tells us, God has given us wisdom on par with Solomon.

If we let it, pride will eagerly take over our sermons. It has no interest in God's glory or in souls being convicted of sin and finding salvation in Christ. Pride would rather help us tickle the ears of listeners because pride fears man and not God. It would rather that we tell a hilarious joke or give an impressive illustration than speak hard truths. It prefers that we be more clever than direct.

Pride makes you the hero of your own sermon, instead of Christ. He is left in the shadows, as pride takes center stage and delights in the accolades of our superior wisdom and skillful communication techniques. Pride thrives when our people tell us how great we are—maybe even the best preacher in the area. It sings that other pulpits have saved their thousands but we our tens of thousands!

And don't think that pride only shows up in our best moments. How do you feel when no one comments on a given sermon when you were sure you knocked it out of the park? After the service, everyone is talking about the rainy day outside, or what they are going to eat for lunch, rather than about your exceptional message. You thought you hit a home run, but they are acting like you grounded out to first.

Don't assume that your injured pride is evidence of your great humility. When your pride is injured, that is a sure sign it is still very much alive. It will get well soon and return to calling the shots. It will say, "Your message *was* great, but these 'are a stiff-necked people'!" (Exod. 32:9). Pride is relentless and must not be merely wounded. It must be slain.

But how do we go about slaying this great beast? I find it fascinating that Christ could demand total allegiance from his followers without an ounce of pride. He actually "humbled himself by becoming obedient to death—even death on a cross!" (Phil. 2:8). In his humanity, Christ did not exalt himself. He allowed God to exalt him and give him "the name that is above every name" (Phil. 2:9). Is there not a message here that we can take with us to the pulpit? We must cling to the cross in our sermon preparation, in our sermon delivery, and in our response to the praise (or criticism) that follows. Once we have "crucified the flesh" (Gal. 5:24) and put to death our old enemy pride, we will be ready to see God work.

I'm sure there have been many times when you, like me, thought you had delivered an absolutely anointed message, only to find that no one seemed moved by what you said. Then there are other weeks when you crawl down from the pulpit knowing you bombed royally and look for a place to hide. But then, a few days later, you get a note from someone saying his life was changed by the sermon you thought was a dud. Oh, and not only that, but he had brought a friend to church who ended up giving his life to Christ. These are the kinds of things that *should* humble us, for they demonstrate that the power lies not within us but in the gospel, "the power of God that brings salvation to everyone who believes" (Rom. 1:16).

Apart from him, "you can do nothing" (John 15:5). What part of *nothing* don't we understand? It is the *something* we claim to have contributed that feeds pride and gives it strength to lay claim to whatever fruit the Lord brings forth.

Humility, of course, is the opponent of pride and the antidote to its seductive poison. Scripture gives two book-ended statements regarding the subject of humility. One says, "Humble yourselves, therefore, under God's mighty hand, that he may lift you up in due time" (1 Pet. 5:6). The second says, "God opposes the proud but shows favor to the humble" (James 4:6). It is far better to obey the former than to experience the latter. Yet since pride blinds us to our lack of humility, we must rely on the all-seeing eye of God to create it in us and reveal it to us. We ought to pray as David did: "Search me, God, and know my heart; test me and know my anxious thoughts. See if there is any offensive way in me, and lead me in the way everlasting" (Ps. 139:23–24).

So, Pastor, we must take inventory on a regular basis and look for telltale signs that pride is lurking in the shadows. Here are some sample questions we can ask ourselves:

- Was I hurt because no one said anything about a message I preached?
- Did I enter the pulpit with expectations of great, quantifiable results?
- Were there intentional guilt trips subtly woven into the message?

- Am I fully aware of the great privilege of having been called to the gospel ministry, thanking God that "he considered me trustworthy, appointing me to his service" (1 Tim. 1:12)?
- Before I preach, do I pray that God will be glorified?
- When things have gone well, do I find myself puffed up?
- Do I tend to seek out people who will praise me and avoid those who might offer criticism?

If you're a young pastor asking when this monster will finally leave you alone, you'll have to ask someone much older than me. I have learned much about the nature of pride over the years, as I have fought plenty of battles against it myself. But even after a great victory, it isn't long before it surfaces again.

Perhaps the best advice I can give you is to always check your motives. The Scriptures are most clear on what your motive should be: "So whether you eat or drink or whatever you do, do it all for the glory of God" (1 Cor. 10:31). Check your appetite for praise. Check your fear of receiving negative feedback (or no feedback). When the feedback is positive, check your spirit and see whether you are rejoicing because of your need for acceptance or because Christ was exalted.

This battle will not be won overnight. Even when things are going well, pride can sneak in past the night watches when all is quiet, and you can hear its whisper: "You were a real hit today. The people loved you." But there is another voice, and it says, "For who makes you different from anyone else? What do you have that you did not receive? And if you did receive it, why do you boast as though you did not?" (1 Cor. 4:7).

Let's be honest enough to admit that there are strong forces from within that demand praise and acceptance. I find it difficult to believe that even the most mature of saints don't feel a hint of jealousy when someone other than themselves is sought out for counsel. We all feel this pain. It is normal because, as children of Adam, we demand our rights to eat from the tree of the knowledge of good and evil. I hope that during our pilgrimage, we come to see ourselves more as the children of God than the children of Adam. Stay the course and let God be God.

Hypocrisy in the Ministry

It has been said that to be a good pastor you need the strength of an ox, the daring of a lion, the harmlessness of a dove, the gentleness of a sheep, the vision of an eagle, the perspective of a giraffe, the endurance of a camel, the stomach of a horse, the faithfulness of a prophet, the fervor of an evangelist, the tenacity of a bulldog, the wisdom of an owl, the industry of a beaver, the head of a scholar, the hide of a rhinoceros, the heart of a child, and the devotion of a mother.

No wonder so many pastors feel pressure! Who could live up to all of that? As we explore the subject of hypocrisy in ministry, I want to be careful to avoid putting a guilt trip on anyone. Most of our hypocrisy is unintentional and is the result of trying to defend our theological "swim lane," a concept we'll explore further in another chapter.

What pastor has not occasionally driven away from the church parking lot and said to himself, "I wish I were experiencing the victorious Christian life I so eloquently preached on this morning"? A number of years ago *Leadership* magazine had a cartoon showing a pastor sitting at his desk and behind him was an enormous bookshelf with hundreds of books on how to be a victorious Christian. Off to the side of his desk was a miniature bookshelf with four books bearing the title, *Biographies of Victorious Christians.* I laughed hysterically because it so captured the reality of the church and the reality of ministry. Is it wrong to preach on something you are not experiencing? No pastor has ever lived up to all that he preaches. There is, however, a difference between delivering a message here and there that doesn't reflect your present spiritual condition and living a life that is totally inconsistent with your preaching.

The word *hypocrisy* carries a lot of weight. It has nasty connotations. No one wants to be called a hypocrite, and yet probably all of us have preached sermons we knew we weren't personally living up to. We have preached on prayer with holy passion while our own prayer lives were shallow. We have preached about how God provides for those who give generously to the church, while we doubted how we were going to make the next car payment.

Many a pastor has taken inventory of his most recent message only to be reminded by his own conscience that what he just verbalized from the pulpit was not true in his own life. The question at hand is: Is that hypocrisy?

Hypocrisy is often defined as believing one thing while living another. I don't think this is a good definition. I can preach against lying and then tell a lie to a police officer who pulls me over on the way home from church. That doesn't necessarily mean I was being hypocritical, but it can mean I was overtaken with temptation in a sinful moment. Hypocrisy is what the religious leaders did in Jesus's day when they made sure to "disfigure their faces to show others they are fasting" (Matt. 6:16). Hypocrisy is outwardly presenting yourself to be what inwardly you know you are not. Hypocrisy is telling your congregation that playing cards is of the devil, but then going on vacation with college buddies and playing poker until the wee hours of the morning. That is very different from succumbing to temptation. Believing what you preach while momentarily failing to apply it is a far cry from preaching what you don't believe. No pastor will ever be on top of his spiritual game every week. He will have times of dryness just like authors have writer's block—but that doesn't mean they no longer believe in writing.

Over the years, I have gone through many spiritually dry seasons. My prayers never seemed to make it to heaven's throne; they just bounced off the proverbial ceiling. My times in the Word felt like traveling to a foreign land where I didn't understand the language. I've battled jealousy, fear, anxiety, and doubts during difficult seasons. It comes with the territory. But it is in these moments when you may be most tempted to become a hypocrite—or at least *feel* like you are one.

Feelings of hypocrisy will take their toll. They can often be self-inflicted wounds. I am reminded of the man in Mark 9:24 who said to Jesus, "Lord, I believe; help my unbelief!" (NKJV). Who knows what wrestling was going on in his soul that could bring such a contradictory statement? The psalmists frequently cried out with similar sentiments. And many of the prophets seemed to express anger toward God or even question his goodness. Were they all hypocrites?

Pastors are indeed called to a higher standard and to be "above reproach" (1 Tim. 3:2); and yes, we are to "set an example for the believers in speech, in conduct, in love, in faith and in purity" (1 Tim. 4:12); but this should not be so confining that we assume we are being hopelessly hypocritical every time we stumble. To do so would proclaim that we are better than those to whom we preach.

What I have found to be most helpful in periods of dryness is to be honest with your people. I have often said something like this: "The passage before us is a powerful truth. I must admit that I have yet to experience what it says. As a matter of fact, this is one area that I have always struggled with, but my experience neither validates nor invalidates the truth of what God says."

I once preached on the disciplines of reading the Scriptures, spending time in prayer, and meditating. I love the Word and enjoy times of study, and meditation comes as natural as breathing to me. On the other hand, while prayer is powerful and important, it is by far the weakest area of my Christian life. In my sermon, I was honest with my people in letting them know that prayer was the weak link in my spiritual journey, but such an admission does not detract from or dilute the authority of God's Word on the subject. Being up front and honest helps fend off the presence or appearance of hypocrisy.

A phrase I often use with our church is "I'm not there yet." When I exegete a text that says something like, "Do not be anxious about anything" (Phil. 4:6), I add a disclaimer to let them know that I haven't arrived at fully applying the passage in my own life. I am often anxious. This helps my people see that I am vulnerable and that I struggle just like they do. I know I find it hard to relate to believers who project total victory and joy. I want to hear about the fears, doubts, and struggles of mature believers. Your congregation does too.

But what about when the charge of hypocrisy actually fits? One of my greatest struggles is putting my hope in man above my hope in God. When I find out about major Christian figures with a noticeable moral failure, I ask what everyone else does: "How could Marty Morality have been living such a double life?"

My bewilderment is not that Marty fell into sin, but that he had been living a shadowy life for years and years. How can someone stand in the pulpit week after week proclaiming

God's truth and not feel the weight of hypocrisy? When did his conscience take the exit ramp? Hypocrisy is a struggle all pastors deal with. No pastor will perfectly live up to what they proclaim to be true. If we don't acknowledge this from the pulpit, then any failure in our lives will be seen as hypocrisy from those we shepherd. If you know you have been hypocritical, then repentance will allow your conscience to be set free. Keep short accounts with yourself. Take inventory at the end of the day or "through the watches of the night" like King David (Ps. 63:6). Your rest will be sweet knowing your mind and heart have one less burden to carry.

CHAPTER 8

THE PASTOR AND DOCTRINAL DIVISION

E ven though the Bible contains rules, moral boundaries, and theology, it is neither a rule book, a moral handbook, nor a systematic theology book. It is the supreme narrative about the fallenness of man and God's rescue mission of sending Jesus to pay the penalty for man's sin and set him free. That narrative is vast, complex, and filled with strange stories, parables, mysteries, poetry, polemics, discourses, and multiple literary genres, which makes it impossible for any man to interpret it perfectly.

But many Christians, and many pastors, seem to believe they have "cracked the code." They become doctrinal police, strolling the evangelical neighborhoods looking for anyone who disagrees with their view. Those found guilty are hauled into a public forum, via social media, for thousands to read about their alleged transgressions. If this sounds overly dramatic, just go online and look at the comments section of any popular Christian blog or Facebook page and watch the napalm that is dropped on those who hold the "wrong" views. Such vitriol defames the name of Jesus, yet it is all supposedly under the guise of trying to "contend for the faith that was once for all entrusted to God's holy people" (Jude 3). The context in Jude, however, has to do with salvation, not exposing and shaming anyone who fails a doctrinal litmus test. Today, every word is put under a microscope and analyzed with scrutiny. This has caused untold division within the body of Christ. Reputations have been slandered and sabotaged by other believers.

There is a song called "They Will Know We Are Christians by Our Love." Unfortunately, experience and observation often tell a different story. Sometimes it seems more accurate to say that they will know we are Christians by our bigotry, moral superiority, hypocrisy, and infighting. Many have been disillusioned and left the church because of this and have found refuge in the arms of humanists who appear to show more love and compassion than the church squabbling over man-made theological systems.

The Spirit searches "the deep things of God." Can he use scholars and their knowledge of Hebrew and Greek? Absolutely. Can he use a new believer to discover a truth or insight that scholars have missed? Certainly. Humility in the church must lead the way, starting with the pastor but extending to the whole congregation. Unity is the fruit of corporate humility.

What Is Your Swim Lane?

Pastor, why do you believe what you believe about the Bible? When you responded to the gospel, you entered a theological "swim lane." What I mean is that when you came to faith, you were discipled by another believer, or started attending a church, or found a blog that resonated with you. Once you felt safe in that particular environment, you inherited a set of beliefs. Whatever your experience, you discovered some wonderful truths about the Bible and the Christian life, but I can assure you that not all of what your swim lane teaches is true.

Don't get me wrong here: all gospel-believing swim lanes will get you to the other end of the pool. If you get some of the secondary doctrines wrong, as we all will, that does not mean you are out of the kingdom. This is very good news! If we truly believe that Jesus is Lord, that he died for our sins, and that he was resurrected on the third day, then "God raised us up with Christ and seated us with him in the heavenly realms in Christ Jesus" (Eph. 2:6). It's a done deal.

Still, we are all in a swim lane of one sort or another, and each lane claims to have the purest interpretation of Scripture. Simple logic says we can't all be right. Each lane has particular beliefs that are distinct from other lanes; thus we set up lane dividers. *Well, I am swimming in the true lane—the rest may be good, but they are a bit polluted with false teaching.* Is that how you are tempted to think? Are you afraid to go under the divider and learn from the guy swimming in the next lane, lest you be labeled a heretic or, worse, a compromiser who is diluting sound doctrine?

We have all been influenced by a myriad of factors such as the way we were raised, the church we grew up in (or didn't grow up in), our friends and professors, and books and blogs that we have read. Our personal experiences with believers and unbelievers have shaped what we believe about the Bible, and when we end up in different swim lanes, there may come a temptation toward friction and conflict, often fueled by pride. Where humility is lacking, grace is lacking, and where grace is lacking, theology becomes lifeless information.

And we wonder why so many people leave the faith or refuse to join. If you disagree on any one of ten thousand issues, you may be labeled a heretic. I have never believed the Bible more passionately than I do today, but I have never had less confidence in man's interpretation of it.

Is it possible that each swim lane has both truth and error? Could it be that we could all learn from one another? Perhaps with such an approach, genuine errors would surface like scum that could be filtered and discarded.

I recently listened to an interview with a very conservative scholar who had done her doctrinal dissertation on the third of the Ten Commandments: "You shall not take the name of the LORD your God in vain" (Exod. 20:7 NKJV). She put hundreds of hours of research into that one sentence and unearthed twenty-three different interpretations.[2] Perhaps some of those views complemented one another, but one thing is certain: the best of scholars don't see eye-to-eye on biblical interpretation of even one simple sentence.

I must have heard more than a dozen interpretations of the Sermon on the Mount. What are we to make of this? What good is the Bible if there are potentially hundreds of thousands of ways to interpret it? Doesn't that give skeptics the right to say, "That's just your interpretation"? If that doesn't bother you, it should. Still, over the years, I have become less disturbed by such diversity of thought. Let me explain.

We must realize that the Bible cannot possibly be perfectly understood or interpreted by everyone equally. Thus, we can expect a certain amount of disagreement. The question is not about whether we disagree, but about *how* we disagree. The only right way to disagree is *humbly*. "God resists the proud, but gives grace to the humble" (James 4:6 NKJV). According to Paul's letter to Titus, grace is an instructor that "teaches us to say 'no' to ungodliness and worldly passions, and to live self-controlled, upright and godly lives" (Titus 2:12).

Paul also acknowledged that "I worked harder than all of them—yet not I, but the grace of God that was with me" (1 Cor. 15:10). Humility should steer any scriptural or doctrinal dispute, and humility does not come without God's grace.

There is so much to discover about Jesus. We can all learn from one another, but only if the lane dividers are removed. As long as we think that our confessional view is *the way, the truth, and the life*, we forfeit the benefit of what others in the body have to offer. People all over the world have experienced Jesus in ways that our intellectual, Western mindset may refuse to accept.

I seriously doubt that those being persecuted for their faith around the world debate issues like Calvinism versus Arminianism, young earth versus old earth, cessationist versus continuationist. I have had the great privilege of meeting so many people from other nations who are living profoundly victorious lives but have never heard of those debates. Still, many present-day American theologians would have you think your church and family will fall apart if you don't land on the right side of such issues.

This is by no means to suggest that we toss out sound doctrine. But defining what is "sound" is not always easy. Clearly, the death, burial, and resurrection of Jesus is the rock upon which we stand. The fact that he is coming again is the rock upon which we find hope. The clear definition of marriage is the rock upon which society is held together. The steadfast love and mercy of God is the rock that we cling to in times of suffering. Beyond that, the waters get murky.

One Word, Many Applications

Though all illustrations break down to some degree, let me offer this one to help us think through the issues of interpretation and application.

I am married and have four children. Imagine we're all sitting around the fire at Christmas while the grandkids play in the basement. One of my children says, "Dad, tell us about your favorite Christmas memory when you were a kid." I give it a moment of thought as I rummage through the attic in my rusty brain in search of the requested memory.

Then, I launch into my reflection of years gone by. There was the time my dad was overseas fighting in the Korean War. The rest of the family was decorating the tree at home with such extravagance it would have made Macy's proud. While standing back and admiring our work of art, the tree toppled over. We all wished that Dad had been there to rescue us from this disaster, but we managed to reassemble it and all was well.

Question: Did my wife and our four children hear the same story? Yes. They could all recite the details, but each would have been affected differently. Why? Because all of them know me differently through their experience and their daily interactions of life. They can't help but have a different interpretation of my reflections on Christmas as a kid, even though all of them have a personal relationship with me.

Jesus has no human flaws, but make no mistake, he is still seen and understood differently based on many factors. From the pastor to the pew-sitter, from the scholar to the school child, from the mother to the maid, we all see and understand him through eyes and ears affected by our experiences and tainted by our fallenness. Church history is filled with interpretive differences in reading his infallible Word through fallible eyes and ears. That history has, tragically, seen doctrinal disputes lead to everything from broken relationships and divided churches to murder and even war.

Yet is it possible, without sounding heretical, that the Lord speaks to all of his children differently, even though we are reading the same book? Is it possible that the underground church in China finds a different emphasis when reading some of Jesus's parables than we do? Does this necessarily mean the meanings are contradictory? No more contradictory than my children interpreting my Christmas memory differently.

Or to bring this to modern-day America, consider the issue of children's education. A homeschool apologist might quote Deuteronomy 6, which teaches that we are to "talk about [God's commands] when you sit at home" (v. 7), while the public-school crowd could quote Mark 16, which tells us we are to "go into all the world and preach the gospel to all creation" (v. 15). Meanwhile the Christian school group heralds forth Psalm 1, which tells us not to be under "the counsel of the ungodly" (1:1 NKJV). Must only one of these be right and the others wrong? Or could the Lord have such a personal relationship with believers that he leads each family to do what is best for their own children, with the support of Scripture for all of them?

As another example, the book of Proverbs offers many positive promises. The formula is: "You do this and God will do this." But in Ecclesiastes, the same writer says, in effect, "I did that and it didn't work." Is one infallible book contradicting another infallible book? No, Proverbs is stating general principles for life, while Ecclesiastes is revealing that these principles don't work in every situation in a fallen world. A "gentle answer" does not *always* turn away wrath (Prov. 15:1) any more than training up a child in "the way he should go" (Prov. 22:6 NKJV) is a promise that you will *never* see rebellion.

In another example, try to imagine facing a very powerful and wise enemy. You seek direction from your commander-in-chief, but his instructions are interpreted by endless numbers of leaders who are all certain they know exactly what he has directed his army to do. Infighting begins and different smaller armies form, which splinter into even smaller armies. Yet all claim allegiance to the supreme commander. Ultimately, they have no chance of victory because they have declared war on one another, all while claiming they are on the same side.

Now suppose all the leaders come together and find out what each one knows about the commander-in-chief. All have had private meetings and unique experiences with him, learning how he thinks and how to interpret aspects of his instructions. As they humbly gather and share their thoughts, the pieces begin to fall into place and instructions become clear. The desire to learn his ways through humility will never displease the "Supreme Commander."

Or to think of it another way, imagine reading a novel and finding it confusing and containing apparent contradictions. You might ask a friend who has read the same book to clarify it for you. They may have noticed the same things, so they offer what they think are solutions to the problem. But those solutions don't match yours. The truth is, you would rather just talk to the author. He could clarify everything. After all, he's the only one who really understands the entire narrative of what is presented and the subtle nuances in his writing style.

The problems inherent with interpreting the Bible are legion, since our background, environment, culture, theological bias, and scores of other issues can work as a filter in our understanding. Does the Bible itself give us any instruction for how to understand it? I believe it does. I believe God has given us clear instructions on how to interpret his Word. Unfortunately, our biases, our swim lanes, and other strong influences often hinder the guiding light of God's Spirit.

In Psalm 119:18, we find David crying out to God to open his Word and teach him the deep things of the Scriptures. He says, "Open my eyes that I may see wonderful things in your law." To make such a cry clearly indicates how David needed the Lord to be his instructor. He knew there were deep truths buried within the text not available to human reason, interpretation, or careful exposition. This is why Proverbs tells us to search for wisdom as we would a "hidden treasure" (Prov. 2:4).

When David asked God to open his eyes, he was not asking for physical eyes to be opened but spiritual eyes. David knew that he had to have spiritual illumination to understand the deep things of God; otherwise his prayers were in vain. These are the types of prayers we must offer before we enter into a study of the Word. I have met many believers who have little or no formal education in biblical studies, yet they have profound insight that seems to go well beyond the recommended methods of exegesis and hermeneutics. Only through a cry to God with an open and humble heart can this be accomplished. God does not share his deepest thoughts with proud pastors, scholars, or church members. He is interested in those who really want to know the truth by laying aside their personal biases and swim lanes.

In the New Testament, we see similar statements. The apostle Paul made it very clear that "my message and my preaching were not with wise and persuasive words, but with a demonstration of the Spirit's power" (1 Cor. 2:4). In other words, Paul simply said that he needed to rely on God to give him clear revelation when he preached. In this same chapter in 1 Corinthians, Paul clearly states that natural human senses are not the place from which we derive revelation. They may help us get through life on a daily basis, but they can never probe the depths of biblical truth. "What no eye has seen, what no ear has heard, and what no human mind has conceived—the things God has prepared for those who love him—these are the things God has revealed to us by his Spirit" (1 Cor. 2:9–10). There is revelation that must be given to us only by God himself. Certainly context, language studies, and hermeneutical principles all play a role, but they can never replace the teaching and illumination of God's Spirit.

We rightly refer to Christianity as a personal relationship with our Savior. If it truly is *personal*, then each one of us knows the Lord in unique and different ways. The scholar knows the Lord through careful study, but not all of us have that kind of mind or the time to pursue such intellectual endeavors. Others know him through deep and intimate prayer, while others may find him through meditation. When we see our personal relationship as the only correct one, we become unteachable and miss what others can teach us about God.

As we seek to train others, let us not forget that training goes both ways. Some of the greatest American scholars and pastors could sit at the feet of uneducated believers on the banks of the Amazon and learn much of Christ. I know this from experience because I go to the Amazon every year to teach and often leave being taught. As I go up and down the river shepherding jungle pastors, I always tell them two things: First, I let them know that they are my heroes. Secondly, I tell them that I may know more about the Bible in a theological and technical sense, but many of them know Jesus better than I do.

Navigating Doctrinal Divides

Even though we all have our own swim lanes and don't know everything about the Scriptures, pastors still need to teach our people and help them navigate through often murky doctrinal waters. As you know, there are endless issues that affect how we understand the Bible and how we operate our churches.

For example, is there a singular type of church polity that produces more mature believers than others? If so, which church government is the most successful? Is there a litmus test?

Do hymns prepare a heart to hear the preached Word better than contemporary praise music? Where does the Bible teach us that preaching must follow congregational singing? Do the Scriptures extol the benefits of a choir? What about a worship team? Is it okay to worship with only a song leader and a piano? A cappella?

Does expository preaching produce stronger believers than topical preaching? If so, how many verses a week should be exposited? Can I teach through a whole chapter at once, or will that water down the Word? Should I take just a few verses each week, even if it takes several hundred years to preach "the whole counsel of God" (Acts 20:27 NKJV)? To what extent must my sermon take into account the cultural dynamic? Would I alter my sermon if it were delivered one week to a sophisticated group in Manhattan and the next week to a coal-mining town in West Virginia? Or should I give the same message to both, resting on the passage that says his Word "shall not return . . . void" (Isa. 55:11 NKJV)?

Should a Baptist support a Presbyterian missionary? Can a cessationist support a continuationist? If not, why not?

Will I hear, "Well done, good and faithful servant" (Matt. 25:23) if I am amillennial? What if I am premillennial? What if I have never heard of either? Am I held accountable? How do I know which is true when many mature believers don't subscribe to the same view? Are they really mature? Does anyone know?

I could go on and on, but you get the point. If you are wondering about my view of Scripture, I hold to the absolute inerrancy, infallibility, and authority of Scripture—but not to man's absolute authority to interpret it. All the subjects above, and many more, have split churches and destroyed relationships. Is it any wonder the world looks at the church and says,

"I think there are far better options than joining such a dysfunctional group of people"?

Not everyone thinks like I do, of course, but I don't like loose ends, and much of Scripture is filled with loose ends, enigmas, paradoxes, mysteries, conundrums, and parables that will never lend themselves to complete clarity this side of heaven. Even if you study for years in the finest seminaries, learn all of the original languages, and fully immerse yourself in ancient Middle Eastern thought and customs, you may still miss the meaning of a text, while God reveals its depth to a little old lady during her morning devotions.

Our human nature says, "I'm right and you're wrong." Here is a bit of advice: *Don't be dogmatic where there is no dog.* Much biblical doctrine is nuanced, and we want clarity. Yet striving to find that clarity has caused endless division over the centuries. Pride can lead to something I call "doctrinal legalism," which is when doctrine is hard to define but we define it anyway and do so with great certainty. When we force clarity beyond what the Spirit has shown us, this is a recipe for divisiveness.

A Humble Solution

What is the only answer to all of this tension? Humility, humility, humility. The Bible is extremely complex and seen through the lens of complex people, which leads to many varied interpretations. God is the only one who knows exactly why he has written everything he has written and exactly what it all means. This does not preclude careful study, careful exposition, or hermeneutical principles, but we must realize that these in and of themselves are limited. Only God can reveal the deep meaning buried in his Word. It comes down to this: if we desire to be the generation that is the answer to Jesus's prayer that we "may be one" (John 17:11), then we will need to pursue humility with great zeal.

As pastors, we must be an example of humility for our people in how we approach God's Word. As we close this chapter, here are a few important guidelines to keep in mind as you study, meditate, and teach.

> **Approach the Word with all the reverence of approaching God himself.** "But on this one will I look: On him who is poor and of a contrite spirit, and who trembles at My word" (Isa. 66:2 NKJV).

> **Approach the Word prayerfully.** "Cause me to understand the way of your precepts, that I may meditate on your wonderful deeds" (Ps. 119:27).

> **Approach the Word with a pure heart.** "If I had cherished sin in my heart, the Lord would not have listened" (Ps. 66:18).

> **Approach the Word with the expectation that you will hear from God.** "Open my eyes

that I may see wonderful things in your law"
(Ps. 119:18).

Approach the Word with the full understanding that you will obey what it says.
"Teach me, LORD, the way of your decrees,
that I may follow it to the end" (Ps. 119:33).

God has given these passages to us as a gift so that we might understand how we are to present ourselves "to God as one approved, a worker who does not need to be ashamed and who correctly handles the word of truth" (2 Tim. 2:15). There is much he wants to teach us that goes far beyond Bible college or seminary. Every time we open his Word, we have an opportunity to sit down and have the Lord be our instructor.

CHAPTER 9

THE PASTOR AND THE PEOPLE

When I was a teenager, there were no such things as portable recorders, cassettes, or CDs. The first time I heard my voice was from a reel-to-reel recorder, which few people even owned. I was shocked to find out what I sounded like. I had always felt that my voice was rich and pleasant. But upon hearing it being projected, I vowed never to speak again. In a similar way, our perception of our personalities is often distorted. Maybe you see yourself as warm and friendly, while others perceive you as cold and indifferent. Maybe you fear that you come across as harsh and abrasive, when most people find your words gracious and "seasoned with salt" (Col. 4:6).

Where is this leading us? I want to take you on an important trip where we will visit some unique personality types, which, if you have not yet experienced, you will. Each person you encounter is an assignment from God to build within you patience, tolerance, love, character, and acceptance. They are designed by God to reveal character flaws and shortcomings in your own life. Thus, I encourage you to remain open and teachable as we move forward.

The Insistent Friend

The first person I want to introduce you to is the one who desperately wants to be your best friend. In spite of their motives, which are typically sincere, you will need to be on guard. It has been my experience that these people are often very needy and once they have latched on, any future rejection by you will be costly to your ministry. Because of their apparent effort to find security in their pastor and not their Lord, they may become greatly offended by your perceived insensitivity toward them after they have invested so much in you.

Years ago, a man in our church kept reaching out to me, and though I appreciated what he did, I wasn't naturally drawn to a close friendship with this brother. He "pinged," but I didn't "pong." After a while, he picked up on the fact that we were never going to be close. Bitterness festered, and before I knew it, he was part of a group that was meeting in homes to determine how to remove me.

How do we respond in such instances? I am ashamed to admit that in this situation I failed miserably. I became afraid that years of work would go down the tubes. Would my precious reputation be destroyed? But what saith Scripture? "I [Jesus, not Mike Minter] will build my church" (Matt. 16:18).

If you are presently experiencing such an individual—and they are in every church—step back and allow God to be your defender. He loves his church more than you and I ever will, and if he wants it to decrease, it will decrease. If he wants it to increase, it will increase. Our concern is to remain faithful.

The Complainer

The next person you will encounter has an opinion on everything and a solution for nothing. Nothing is ever right in the church. They seem to live life looking for things or people to complain about. They will drain the very life out of you, sharing their opinions in letters, notes, scribblings on the back of the bulletin, emails, voicemails, and any other form of communication known to man. So how do we respond?

This is a great opportunity to minister. Do not do it in writing. I know it is quicker and easier and less intimidating to fire off a quick email response, but any correction in writing is left wide open for misinterpretation. Always meet one-on-one and try to lead them to see their critical nature. You can be sure that it manifests itself in every relationship they have. If you don't tell them how they are coming across, who will? Yes, you run the risk of having them become offended or leave the church, but what is the loss if they refuse to change? "Wounds from a friend can be trusted, but an enemy multiplies kisses" (Prov. 27:6).

The Born Leader

The next type of person may also be the most prevalent: the strong personality. I would guess that they make up about 10 percent of your church body. These are people who, if guided by the Spirit, will do great work for the kingdom. They are extremely valuable to the ministry, but it can be disastrous if they rise to leadership too quickly.

There are several common denominators that tend to characterize these people. They are born leaders and used to winning. Failure is not in their vocabulary. They are competitive and may view ministry like a sport. "My Bible study is the biggest one in the church." Their flesh is very accomplished at getting its way. With all their strengths, they can also be easily offended and don't always respond well to correction. They are often impatient and are easily frustrated when ministry doesn't show signs of growth *now*!

Those traits may seem bad, but if yielded to the Spirit, they become great assets to the church. Before ever putting one of these people in positions of leadership, which they will aspire to, make sure you see evidence of the fruit of the Spirit of God at work in their lives, otherwise you will be in for a great deal of trouble. *Always pick humility over ability!* The temptation for any pastor is to look for powerful, successful people who have achieved a great deal in the secular world and assume they can help transfer these same skills into the kingdom. May I tell you, with the experience of four decades of ministry: *That is not how God works.* "But God chose the foolish things of the world to shame the wise; God chose the weak things of the world to shame the strong" (1 Cor. 1:27).

Let me tell you what can happen. These people often have, for years, used human methods to achieve human results. Once they step into kingdom work, God begins to do *his* work. One of his favorite words is *wait*—a word that is foreign to the strong, successful personality. Such a person is not used to taking orders from a higher authority—he has always been the authority. He may try even harder to get things moving. New programs emerge, more meetings are scheduled, more people are pulled in, more emails are sent, and more labor-intensive efforts based on human methodology begin to surface. "For the wisdom of this world is foolishness in God's sight. As it is written: 'He catches the wise in their craftiness'" (1 Cor. 3:19).

The kingdom of God does not work on man's terms. So when results don't manifest as some of these folks have experienced in the business world, they sense failure. They run for cover, and that cover is usually found in another church. Here is what I have found: Very strong people in the world can become very weak in the kingdom if not shepherded well. Spiritual warfare is too much for them to take. If they are not walking in the Spirit, they will use the carnal weapons of this world, which will always fail.

The kingdom of God works on a different time schedule ("wait"), a different set of principles (biblical ones), and a different power structure (the Holy Spirit). Why does God do everything in reverse of how we think? So that he, not man, will get the glory. "Let the one who boasts boast in the Lord" (1 Cor. 1:31).

But let's not throw the baby out with the bathwater. I know many strong personalities who walk in the Spirit in all humility of mind. They fear God and never desire to move ahead of him. I work with many of them daily.

Strong people who walk in the Spirit will have their strength removed, and weak people who walk in the Spirit will become strong because God's "power is made perfect in weakness" (2 Cor. 12:9). The apostle Paul is the quintessential strong personality whom God humbled on the road to Damascus.

As an aside, pastors are often very strong personalities who may be tempted to use worldly methods to build the church. A church can be large, but that doesn't automatically mean God's hand of blessing is upon it. If you are a pastor or church leader, ask yourself a hard question: "Why do people come to our church?" If a survey were taken, what would they say? Would you hear things like, "I love the location," "The sermon makes me feel uplifted every week," "The preacher has a really great sense of humor," or "The music is performed so professionally"?

Dear friend, may I be so bold as to tell you that none of these are valid reasons for your church to grow. Do you remember the words of the woman at the well? "Come, see a man who told me everything I ever did. Could this be the Messiah?" (John 4:29).

More than fifty years ago, A. W. Tozer gave this convicting assessment, which rings even more true today:

> It is now common practice in most evangelical churches to offer the people, especially the young people, a maximum of entertainment and a minimum of serious instruction. It is scarcely possible in most places to get anyone to attend a meeting where the only attraction is God. One can only conclude that God's professed children are bored with Him, for they must be wooed to meeting with a stick of striped candy in the form of religious movies, games and refreshments.[3]

Christ must be the main attraction, and if anyone or anything else is at the center of worship and preaching, it is not of God. Now that I have angered some of you, I would ask you to reflect on the Scriptures and see if this is not so, "for since in the wisdom of God the world through its wisdom did not know him, God was pleased through the foolishness of what was preached to save those who believe" (1 Cor. 1:21). The ultimate compliment you could ever receive as a pastor is that you preach Christ and the hard, unvarnished truth of Scripture.

So, whether you are a strong personality or not, ask the Lord to make you, and all of the leaders in your church, humble servants who are submitted to the guiding of the Holy Spirit.

The Painful Departures

I could name a lot of painful things that have happened over my years of ministry, and it would be hard to single out the one that hurt the most. Watching a small child die of leukemia is about as hard as it gets. Seeing a couple's marriage dissolve ranks high. Watching a young prodigal wallow in the pigpen of fraternity life at college and vicariously feeling what his parents are feeling is certainly discouraging. In all of those situations, you feel the pain others are experiencing.

Perhaps the most difficult part of ministry is the loss of good friends. Every pastor will experience this. Could there be anything more devastating to a shepherd than to see his beloved sheep, whom he has dearly loved, depart for better grassland? The jealousy and anger that launched the spear of Saul, had it struck its target (1 Sam. 19:10), would have inflicted less pain upon David than had Jonathan withdrawn his friendship.

Some pastors may be more socially connected to their people than others. But no matter your personality, the loss of friends over ministry disputes carries with it a hurt all its own.

Good friends set out to start a church and advance the kingdom. Your hopes are high and the strategy sessions are a blast. Everything looks great on paper. Plans are made, goals are set, and the unity of spirit couldn't be stronger. However, people are tested in the crucible of experience, and the dross of character surfaces when the fire heats up. You begin to see those friends in a different light. You become surprised at their knee-jerk reactions, while you remain perfectly calm. Can't they see the big picture? Why can't they see things as clearly as you do? Their weaknesses are exposed, and you are quick to point out those weaknesses, which only strains the relationship all the more. You begin to see yourself as the righteous judge, who only has a few minor flaws (if any). You couldn't possibly be at fault. The rift becomes so great that, inevitably, one of you must leave. The once-great friendship is severed, and the pain is excruciating. You spend hours reliving everything that happened. You play back the film a thousand times, but the story is always the same—you were right, and they were wrong.

But because you were the one who took the video, you are not in the picture. Others, however, are shooting their own videos and will see things very differently than you do and—to borrow a technical term—it's all in high definition. Your intransigence and refusal to admit your faults will surface, and that may cause you to lose even more friends and church members.

To be sure, every leader has flaws, sinful behavior, and shortcomings that will be highlighted over time. Sinful behavior must be dealt with, of course, but *inability* in leadership cannot be fixed quite so easily. Trying to make someone into something they are not is like trying to get a person who is tone deaf to sing on key—they just don't have the ability.

I learned early in the game that I was not a great visionary. The pressure of ministry exposed this shortcoming as I found myself in many leadership meetings without a clear vision to bring to the table. Try as I would, my mind simply wouldn't go down that path. I soon became a pawn in the hands of every strong personality in the church. Someone would say, "Mike, you need to take the church in this direction," while another would tell me something totally different. I felt like a wishbone. Don't get me wrong: I am very strong in the pulpit and can speak with great passion about the things in Scripture that have forged a conviction in my heart. But I don't think the Bible is clear on the perfect ministry philosophy, so I tend not to be passionate about my own.

Good leaders will decide on a course of action and set sail in spite of the wind's direction. I have hurt too many people, however, by leading our vessel halfway across the ocean and then being convinced that we are on a bad course and need to change direction or head back to shore. This frustrates visionaries to no end. They have invested hours working with you to shape a vision for the church, and now you are steering the ship somewhere else. This causes people to leave angry, hurt, and frustrated.

Other personality types get the same results but for different reasons. These are the strong, take-the-hill kind of leaders. A pastor like this will not give up on his vision, no matter the opposition. People begin to see him as a proud, demanding, "my way or the highway" kind of leader. Even his friends may feel like they aren't being listened to, and they, too, will make their exit.

Another scenario that can breed conflict is when a staff member is dismissed or a member of the body is disciplined.

No matter how it is explained, if the person is not in full agreement with the leadership's decision, their attitude will leak out and poison many against you as the pastor. You're stuck. If you explain the situation in too much detail, you risk damaging the person's reputation. If you say too little, you could be accused of hiding information, which is translated as lying. This can lead to people taking sides, and before you know it, more friends have departed.

Departures are painful under any circumstances, but they are particularly painful when you know that good people have left for bad reasons. Maybe they listened to a biased report, believed it, and left. Your desire will be to chase after them and set the record straight, but reopening old wounds does not always end well. If their departure felt like losing an arm, pursuing them may restore your arm—or cause you to lose the other one. There have been times when I pursued only to realize I was going nowhere. It is best to first examine the maturity of the one who left. Proverbs reminds us that "he who corrects a scoffer gets shame for himself" (9:7 NKJV), which is exactly what happened to me in several instances.

On the other hand, if you have high regard for the one leaving, then it is worth the pursuit, with all the passion you can muster. One of the key issues is taking inventory of anything you may have contributed to their departure. If you are guilty, then seek forgiveness. This breaks down walls faster than a battering ram.

Keeping a Tender Heart

When a pastor is tempted to resent his ministry, or those to whom he is ministering, it is time to reassess his calling. He must take inventory of his gifts, talents, and priorities. So much of what we are called to become can be distorted because seeds of bitterness begin to take root (Heb. 12:15). I have seen many a pastor who is at war with his people. He wants to bring them into submission to his personal agenda and becomes frustrated when that agenda fails. The calling becomes a job, and the ministry loses its spiritual dimension. We may take on a business mindset and see our people as unpaid employees who should do our bidding.

Moses began to see the people of Israel as a "burden" (Num. 11:11). He developed resentment toward them and toward God. We may be tempted to do the same. I have always been encouraged by reminding myself of all the people in the church who are joyful and supportive of me and the ministry. This has been the vast majority over the years. If we focus on the few who are disgruntled, it will weigh upon our spirits like a ball and chain, hindering any progress.

Still, you must be aware that there will always be people assigned by God to keep you humble. You must keep a tender heart toward them. This is what shepherding is all about. Dealing with those who may never love you back isn't easy, but we can look toward the example of Christ. I once heard it said that all pastors have people in the congregation they want to help out and others they want to help *out*. Our Lord clearly loved the unlovely—lepers, tax collectors, the rich, the poor. Not to mention sinners like you and me. Even for those who put him on the cross, Jesus prayed, "Father, forgive them, for they do not know what they are doing" (Luke 23:34).

I personally believe that difficult people are the ones who need us the most but may love us the least. Ministering to those who praise us and worship the ground we walk on is not difficult, but it can often feed our flesh. I know I am naturally drawn to those who are thankful and appreciate my ministry in their lives. The Bible reminds us of how easy it is to show regard for those who reciprocate it: "If you love those who love you, what reward will you get? Are not even the tax collectors doing that?" (Matt. 5:46).

But Jesus also made clear that "it is not the healthy who need a doctor, but the sick. I have not come to call the righteous, but sinners" (Mark 2:17). People who complain, murmur, and gripe about everything are greatly in need of spiritual help. It can be tempting to wish that they would grace the church down the street with their attendance. We want a congregation free of difficult people, but this is not realistic. Don't forget, sometimes *we* are the difficult people.

We must keep a warm heart toward those who give the cold shoulder. These are people who need our care, as are people who carry the immense weight of life struggles—be they spiritual, physical, financial, or relational.

I was on a men's retreat a few years ago, and a man whom I had never met pulled me aside before lunch and asked if he could speak to me. I must confess, I didn't want to hear any problems—all I wanted was some time to myself and some fellowship around the lunch table. But I said, "Sure, let's talk." We sat down at a picnic table and he began to unload. I thought, *This is going to be a long conversation . . . and I'm going to miss lunch.* I was displaying such great love for the brethren, right? I was consumed by how inconvenienced I was. But as I listened, I began to feel some compassion. Mercy, believe it or not, is one of my spiritual gifts—however, it goes into hibernation during lunch. I started to rebuke myself. *Is stuffing my belly more important than caring for this man?*

To make a long story short, that conversation began a friendship that eventually led me to stand at the altar and officiate this man's wedding. By God's grace, my heart was reoriented away from fulfilling my flesh and toward serving one of God's children. As pastors, we will do well to remember: There are no "off-duty" times when you are around your people.

It can be difficult to maintain a shepherd's heart while facilitating Sunday services and attending strategy meetings. Even study time can take away from time with your people. I know that in the evangelical ranks, there are differing opinions about the role of the teaching pastor—some feel that this is the main calling of their lives and nothing short of thirty to forty hours of preparation is acceptable, while other staff members take care of the weddings, funerals, and hospital visits. I don't pretend to have the final answer on this, but I do know that constant study can keep you from being relevant and fresh.

Many of my illustrations come from everyday life with my people. Balance is important.

Though I can't see everyone, I do frequently visit the hospital to keep my heart in tune with those who are physically hurting. If I stand in the pulpit with great teaching and superior exegesis, while being totally disconnected from the people God has called me to shepherd, then ministry is just a theory. They need to know that you hurt with them. I often visit men in their workplaces and then grab lunch afterward to get a sense of the pressure, time constraints, and commute. This is real life, and we need to bring the Word to bear upon the working world. We need to feel the texture of life in the fast lane while commuting in the slow lane. By coming alongside them in their daily lives, your people will know that you truly care.

Another environment that will keep the flames of compassion burning is small groups. This is where people will pray for you and get to know who you really are. Plus, it is good "PR." The members of your group will spread the word to others that you are just a regular guy facing all the regular-guy problems of life. The pulpit tends to show us in a different light than what we really are because there is a gravity and seriousness that the pulpit rightly conveys. But this is not the real you—or should I say, it isn't *all* of you. When I visit someone's home (and I know I'm a little crazy), within minutes of walking through the door I'll be on the floor wrestling with their kids. I'm not putting on an act—that's the real me. I read them bedtime stories and let them show me their room and toys. I love it! This may not be your personality, but whoever you really are, let your people see it. These encounters keep our hearts warm toward the body.

Even simpler, hang around after each church service and make yourself available for questions. This helps you stay fresh and gives you insight into what kinds of questions people are asking and how your message reached them.

If all of that "people time" sounds overwhelming, that's okay too. It may seem counterintuitive, but sometimes serving your flock with a tender heart requires getting away for a while. Perhaps that is why Jesus, from time to time, broke away from the crowds to be alone with the Father (Matt. 14:23). You need time to refuel. You need time away.

I know that enjoying a week on the beach or in the mountains isn't always feasible, especially in the early days of ministry when funds are tight. I remember when Kay and I were getting started and had very little money. I can't tell you the number of times I heard people say to me something like, "Mike, we just got back from a cruise to Bermuda; you really need to take a break and surprise the family. Here is some literature on the cruise line." I would stare into the faces of these well-meaning people with a smile, all the while wondering how I would even pay for new windshield wipers on my car that had 150,000 miles on it.

I am now at a place where I can take a nice trip occasionally, but many pastors can't. Regardless, you still need rest. Let your people know that you are taking some time off to be with your family and that you will not be available. There are others who can carry the load in your stead for a brief season. By no means should you despair that you can't take a luxurious vacation. There are others within your church who are struggling financially and have no place to go. There are missionaries who only come home every four years. As you already know, our calling is one of sacrifice, and thus we may not possess the same material abundance as others. That is no reason to fret, but it is a reminder that we should lead in the example of how not to "love the world or anything in the world" (1 John 2:15).

CHAPTER 10

THE PASTOR AND CRITICISM

Criticism is one of the most difficult challenges of ministry. Many pastors have quit because the pain of criticism is too much to bear. All criticism is hard, but it is particularly hurtful when it comes from those you shepherd.

Pastoral ministry sometimes feels like a spectator sport. It is one of the few professions where you go to work in front of large crowds. Everyone is watching you and grading you, or at least it feels that way. Your performance cannot be hidden behind your résumé or education. Those in your congregation couldn't care less about your doctorate from seminary, but they want to know if you will deliver the goods on Sunday morning. In this chapter, we will talk about the different forms of criticism and how a God-fearing pastor can respond well.

Criticism's Many Faces

Since people are very unique in their makeup, their methods of critique will take on manifold expressions. Here are a few examples.

First, there is what I call the *cowardly* critic. This is the individual who sends you a nasty letter, or writes on the back of the bulletin a nitpicky correction to your sermon, but doesn't sign it. Nothing leaves a pastor feeling more defrauded than unsigned criticism. I once quoted three times from A. W. Tozer over a period of two months. Someone took the bulletin and scratched out the word "Bible," so the bulletin read, Reston Tozer Church. Even as I type these words, I'm steamed just thinking about how cowardly some people can be.

Let's move on to the *guilty without a jury* critic. He assumes he has all the facts and drops the gavel, pronouncing you "Guilty!" on all five charges. These people are just one notch above the coward. They pass judgment without giving you a hearing. Their questions are accusatory: "Why did you lie in your sermon last week?" They are active indictments on you and your character. Rather than bringing an accusation, the critic could say, "I certainly don't have all the facts, but it appears that what you said last week from the pulpit is inconsistent from your previous stand. Could you email me at your convenience and tell me if I'm off track?"

Then there is the *I'm ready to explode* critic. This person does not keep short accounts but allows things to stack up over the years and then vents it all in one letter or meeting. You will be shocked at how they have been feeling about you all these years. Your soul gets one long blast from the furnace. You get third-degree burns and wonder how anyone could have so much stored-up anger toward you. You may begin thinking through your relationship history trying to figure out where the wheels came off.

Allow me to give a bit of advice on handling a critic like this. Years ago, a lady came into my office and let me have it. There are times when the critic is right and we need to own up to the truth of their criticism, but that was not the case with this woman. After I listened to her accusation, this word popped into my mind: *perception*. If I disagreed with her it would come across as defensive, but if I agreed with her I would be lying. Here is the question I asked: "What in my actions or words have caused you to perceive me the way you do?" This question avoids admitting guilt and skirts defensiveness. Once she gave me her answer, I then knew what corrections I needed to make to avoid her perception of me. Try it. It has been a lifesaver.

On more than one occasion, I have had people make an appointment so they could unload their disappointment with me face-to-face. Though these are often the most hurtful sessions, at least they give you a chance to interact in-person. I have often had to endure two-hour sessions with people who arrive with a manila folder with my name on it. Oh, the joy of having people pull out several typed-up pages listing all your faults, from how you preach, to your lack of compassion.

However, allow me to take a break here and state that many others have met with me for the sole purpose of encouraging me by being gentle and gracious in their critique. Those are the people who give me strength to stay the course.

By now you're probably wondering what kind of a tyrant I must be to have experienced so much criticism. Truth be told, I am very well-loved by our people. It's not hard to get a meeting with me, even though I have a large congregation. I am not an intimidating personality, so there is little fear in confronting me. This can be good and bad. I trust you know yourself well enough to know how you are perceived. Much of what I am relating in this book is obviously centered around my personality—what may crush me might have little effect on you, and vice versa. The common denominator for all of us is that no one likes criticism, even the constructive type. It leaves the soul raw and tender. When we come under criticism, we find ourselves morose, depressed, and even short-tempered toward those we love.

Navigating Criticism

When criticism comes, it isn't always easy to think clearly or receive the feedback in a biblical way. Here are a few things you can think about during those moments.

Did he or she try to hurt me with their criticism? Most people are not intentionally cruel, so I can usually rule this out. People in your congregation may not understand how painful criticism can be to a pastor.

Was I overly sensitive to the criticism? This is usually a greater possibility than someone's intentional cruelty toward you.

Does the critic have my best interest in mind, even if he is not communicating it well? Assuming good intentions on the part of your critic can alleviate unnecessary pain.

Do I view this criticism as assigned by God for my benefit? If I don't, then I will miss an opportunity to grow.

Are there any ways that I have brought offense to the church and should therefore seek forgiveness? Try to make it a habit to periodically and publicly admit to the congregation ways you may have been an offense. This will clear your conscience and teach the body of Christ how to humble themselves in their home or office. It will also show the members of the church that you are human. People relate better to humans than superhumans.

The Sting of the Critic

Our weekly staff meetings are a special time for me. I am extroverted by nature, and I thoroughly enjoy mingling with the team. Meetings are usually uplifting and refreshing for me as I fellowship with those whom God has called me to work with closely. However, once the meeting is over, the dreaded time has arrived. I can't put it off any longer. My mailbox is calling me (not to mention my email). There are letters to be read and correspondence that must be addressed. Sticking my hand into my mail slot is like sticking my hand into a tree hole.

Will I find honey or a bee? Will it be a sweet experience, or will I get stung? As I return to my desk and sort through the mail, I find a few Hallmark cards that are a joy to open. In one, I quickly recognize Sally's impeccable handwriting. Her warm and encouraging words flow off the page and find their way into my heart. Others contain similar grace that encourage my heart and motivate my spirit.

I then notice a large envelope with thirteen stamps staring me in the face. It's addressed to me and just below my name are the words *Personal* and *Confidential*. This is no Hallmark card. But maybe it is an admirer who wants to expound on what a great pastor I have been over the years? That possibility evaporates as I realize by the weight of the envelope that there are at least twelve typewritten pages. Though I think I'm doing a decent job, I know I'm not perfect. Perhaps it's a theological issue they wish to present and simply want my input? Something tells me that this is probably not the case. My fingernail nervously finds its way under the sealed edge and begins to separate the flap from the backside. My heart is racing as I pull the letter from its private cocoon. It starts out, "Dear Mike, we have learned much from you over the years from your fine teaching, and for this we are truly grateful."

Now I'm bracing for the "but."

"But recently, your lack of vision, leadership, and pastoral care has forced us to look elsewhere for fellowship." The rest of the letter is a running commentary on all my character flaws, which, by the way, *everyone* in the congregation is apparently concerned about.

With each page my heart sinks a little more than before. The whole congregation thinks I'm worthless. I might as well move on and spare everyone the pain of having to endure my pathetic leadership any longer. I pull in a close friend on the church staff and have him read the letter, hoping he might see it as just a couple of disgruntled members with a poor attitude. In times like those, you need someone to come alongside and give you hope and strength.

Why does criticism hurt us so deeply? Shouldn't we see it as just another hazard of ministry and move on? No one likes to be criticized, but it comes with the territory in any type of leadership. However, it is very different for a pastor. If you are the head of a company, can an employee send you a letter or email questioning your character and leadership? Not if they want to continue being employed. Can a private in the army blast a general for his incompetence or failure to rally the troops? Not unless he is looking for a court martial. Can a third baseman spread nasty rumors about the coach? Not if he wants to avoid being benched. In ministry, there are no such restraints on our people. They are free to leave a counseling session and tell all their friends that you not only had no answer for their problems, but you also didn't seem to care. You, on the other hand, can say nothing about the session because of the confidential nature of the meetings.

Ministry is upside down from how the rest of the world operates. Does it ever occur to you that you get paid to tell people how bad they are? Meanwhile, you are tempted to sin, just like they are, but you are called to live above reproach.

Someone could be hooked on pornography and still be a qualified surgeon. Someone could go through five marriages and be a great trial lawyer. A carpenter could have a gambling problem but still be masterful with a hammer and nails. Pastors, however, cannot have significant moral flaws and still be an effective minister.

Criticism is not going to chase after the immoral doctor, lawyer, or carpenter because no one really cares about their character, as long as the services you pay for are done in a professional manner. As a pastor, however, we talk about having integrity while seeking to become like Christ. This invites criticism. People will break out the microscope to see what your marriage is like, how your children behave, and whether you are really experiencing the power of God you expound upon each Sunday. That is a lot to live under. We have already talked about hypocrisy, but that is the first criticism that will come if your life is—or is perceived to be—inconsistent with the messages you preach.

I have also come to realize that the pain of criticism is directly proportional to the relationship you have with the person who criticizes you. For example, if you are on your way to work and someone calls you a jerk because you cut them off while changing lanes, you will probably forget the incident by the time you get to the office. But if your father calls you a jerk, you may never forget it. This is why criticism from a brother or sister in Christ is so painful. They are family. You may not know everyone in your congregation well, but their words can cut deeply because of the spiritual relationship that exists through Christ.

Sheep Have Teeth

A number of years ago I had to bring a person into my office to inform him that he was being divisive and sowing seeds of discord within the body. Let this be a warning: tread carefully when offering correction to a gossip. I made sure to have another staff member present for protection, lest I be accused later of being judgmental or unloving. The individual stayed in the church, but he was disengaged for about a year, which allowed bitterness to fester.

Hebrews 12:15 tells us to be careful so that "no bitter root grows up to cause trouble and defile many." Boy, did that passage ever come to life. When he resurfaced, I became the target of a smear campaign. My name and reputation were dragged through the mud. I lost friends, many of whom had come to Christ under my preaching, and a group formed for the sole purpose of running me out of town.

These were dark days, to say the least, and my soul was weary in the battle. I was quickly losing confidence that God would see me through that season. I began to cower and would do anything to keep these people from destroying me. I dragged our elders through meeting after meeting only to see matters get worse. I had officially become a coward, but I felt that years of ministry were at stake. Taking the wrong approach to this might capsize the whole ship. I was led by fear, not faith.

Most of you will experience something like this in your ministry, if you haven't already. Why do people attack us when we have dedicated our lives to benefit their souls? Still, it is inevitable because the enemy is real and people are sinful. In every gospel-centered congregation, the enemy will plant a few troublemakers who will try to break the pastor and push him out. It can be scary wondering when the "fire" of the tongue will begin to rage (James 3:6).

So what should I have done when the walls began closing in? I should have committed myself "to Him who judges righteously" (1 Pet. 2:23 NKJV). There should have been only one meeting, where we entrusted ourselves to God's will. If sharp-toothed sheep wanted to destroy my reputation, then so be it. Wasn't our Savior slandered? He never defended himself, so that God would be his defender. "When they hurled their insults at him, he did not retaliate; when he suffered, he made no threats" (1 Pet. 2:23).

In the congregation where I have served through the years, 95 percent of the folks are kind, loving, and supportive. But as I've already mentioned, God sends certain people our way to keep us humble. How would you handle it if you preached in a huge church, with thousands coming to hear you each week? What would you do if you received constant praise, if everyone always agreed with you, and if your church maintained a large budget that never suffered a shortfall? The truth is that you, or I, would soon forget God. We would see ourselves as indispensable for kingdom growth. You can no doubt think of some big-name pastors who have, sadly, gone down that detrimental path.

In the book of Jonah, it is interesting that in the first chapter, the mariners were said to have thrown Jonah overboard. However, in chapter 2, Jonah says that *God* "hurled me into the depths" (2:3). Or there is Joseph, who told his brothers, "Do not therefore be grieved or angry with yourselves because *you sold me* here; for *God sent me* before you to preserve life" (Gen. 45:5 NKJV, emphasis added).

Both Jonah and Joseph could look back over their difficulties and see that God was behind them all, even though wicked men did their wicked deeds. Remember this, Pastor: *Every criticism that comes your way is ultimately sent by God.* His ways are often hard to understand. The Arminian would say he allowed it, and the Calvinist would say he ordained it. The bottom line is that God could stop any trial or challenge, but sometimes he doesn't. Somehow his seal of approval is on it, and you, my friend, are the recipient of his good pleasure.

I know that God is always behind the scenes working everything out for my good and his glory. It is not always easy to see that amid the turmoil, but haven't we been called to "live by faith, not by sight" (2 Cor. 5:7)?

CHAPTER 11

THE PASTOR AND DISCOURAGEMENT

Another formidable foe in our work of ministry is discouragement. The word simply means "to lose courage," and it shows up in many ways according to our varied personalities and wiring. Among other things, a pastor may become discouraged by doubt, through loneliness, or by playing the comparison game. Let's talk about how to stay the course when times of discouragement inevitably come.

Dealing with Doubt

I don't know about you, but I have a very curious mind. I can't stop inquiring about every question I run across in Scripture. How does hell work? Why did God destroy the Canaanites? Why does evil exist? Why do Bible translations interpret texts differently? And so on. I dig into these issues until I hit rock and then get frustrated because I know it's the end of the journey.

Not everyone is wired like me, of course, but all pastors have questions about how God operates. I certainly do. That doesn't mean I disbelieve the texts, but it does mean I struggle with why there doesn't seem to be more clarity on certain issues.

You might ask how you can even be a pastor when you have so many unanswered questions. Some might answer this way: God is sovereign, so what right do we have to question him? "Does the clay say to the potter, 'What are you making?'" (Isa. 45:9).

Others cling to the ancient mantra, "God said it. I believe it. That settles it." That makes for a great bumper sticker, but when hard times come, it won't give you comfort to press on. The psalmists and prophets didn't have that phrase blazoned on their chariots—those men sometimes came to God with very harsh words. Men of God in the Scripture were often filled with doubts, and I'm so glad they were. I can't relate to people who think they understand everything perfectly.

Learning the ways of God is a lifelong journey. Don't just say, "Well, God is sovereign," and use that as an excuse to shut off your curiosity. There is great reward and joy in seeking to know the mind of God. But how do we live with the struggle of what we don't understand?

For me, it helps to recognize the deep complexity of God's Word, which only comes with time and study. It is a supernatural book, much of it beyond my comprehension, though every day I see its accuracy regarding the human condition. I have a little tagline that I live by: *What I do understand about the Bible convinces me that what I don't understand must have a reasonable explanation.*

I see five categories of information in Scripture, and they may help give you peace of mind when you are tempted to doubt:

1. **Things we will never know.** "The secret things belong to the LORD our God . . ." (Deut. 29:29).

2. **Things we know partially.** "For now we see only a reflection as in a mirror; then we shall see face to face. . . ." (1 Cor. 13:12).

3. **Things that are hard to understand.** Peter comments on Paul by saying, "His letters contain some things that are hard to understand" (2 Pet. 3:16).

4. **Things we are not mature enough to handle as of now.** Jesus said to his disciples, "I have much more to say to you, more than you can now bear" (John 16:12).

5. **Things that are clear.** Paul says that natural revelation reveals clearly what Scripture says about the creator. "For since the creation of the world God's invisible qualities—his eternal power and divine nature—have been clearly seen, being understood from what

has been made, so that people are without excuse" (Rom. 1:20).

This, for me, is a more honest approach to all the difficulties. I don't ignore them with "bumper sticker theology." I face them head-on. There are times when I get a good, satisfactory answer, and there are times when the answers remain shrouded in mystery. I trust you can relate.

We don't tend to do well with mystery. We want answers and certainty. Certainty is an anchor, while mystery is a free-for-all. For this reason (and many others), believers should never idolize their pastor. He should never be put on a pedestal, because pedestals are for statues of those long gone. Bronze and marble men can no longer fall. They are freed from doubts; they "know fully" (1 Cor. 13:12). Those still alive, however, may crash and burn from their lofty positions. Pastors come from the line of Adam and live in a broken world. We are real people with real problems. We sin and have fears over what life may throw our way. We question God when tough times come. Some of us may have more faith than others, but we are all mere men. It has been said that "the best of men are men at best."

One of the things I have tried to do over the years is acknowledge that I have not "arrived" at perfect clarity and wisdom. There are times when I'm not even sure I have gotten out of the gate. It is okay to let your people know that you, like them, are still figuring things out. Hiding your doubts and struggles will force you to put on a mask week after week and pretend to be a superhero. That is not sustainable. But we also don't need to air all our dirty laundry just so we can "relate" to the congregation. You are the pastor. Lead with confident humility. Let the body know that you struggle, but more than that, let them know there is a great and blessed hope.

Loneliness

It has often been said, particularly in the corporate and political worlds, that it is "lonely at the top." We hear related expressions like, "The buck stops here," or, "If you can't stand the heat, get out of the kitchen." But should such sentiments be applied to the pastorate? Have we been called to make unilateral decisions? Do we speak authoritatively like the prophets or kings of old?

I recognize that there are different leadership models within the church. In some congregations, the pastor is the boss and what he says goes. Others have multiple pastors or teachers with cooperative authority. At Reston Bible Church, we are elder-led, which means that we have a shared leadership structure—though many elder-led churches do so more in theory than in reality.

No matter the structure that exists at your church, people tend to complain about leadership. This has always been true. Just read Numbers 14 and see how the disgruntled masses treated Moses and Aaron. They didn't like the way things were going, and they took it out on the leaders God had provided. And here in the modern West, people see the teaching pastor as the "big cheese," whether he likes it or not. So in that sense, it can, indeed, be lonely at "the top" for any pastor.

That loneliness can occur for several reasons. First, we want people to see us as someone they can follow—not just spiritually, but in every other way. We fear being viewed as weak or flawed, lest people not think highly of us. We are expected to demonstrate the way to live in faith, prayer, love, sacrifice, holiness, joy, patience, mercy, peace, wisdom, knowledge, giving, leadership, and any other virtue you can think of. Anything short of this could bring about condemnation and criticism (or so we think), so we either retreat and keep people from truly knowing us, or we put on a mask and pretend. Either way, we are not being true to God, ourselves, or those we lead, and, thus, we find ourselves all alone.

Yet if truth be known, most of your people are not looking for a *perfect* leader but a *genuine* leader to whom they can relate and trust. I have been blessed to find many people over the years who have been able to get to know the real me. They know I am but dust—because God says I am (Ps. 103:14). They know I am fallen—because God says I am (Rom. 3:23). They know I am tempted like all men are—because God says I am (1 Cor. 10:13). These are my credentials as one born of Adam. As a Christian, I am born again and redeemed. As a pastor, I am called to be above reproach, but I will never be perfect this side of glory.

Consider how Paul let us peer into the corners of his life. He said he came to the Corinthians "in weakness with great fear and trembling" (1 Cor. 2:3). He asked for prayer that he might be bold enough to "fearlessly make known the mystery of the gospel" (Eph. 6:19). At times, he had to defend himself against attacks upon his motives and character that brought him "great distress and anguish of heart" (2 Cor. 2:4).

Loneliness does not come only from our position of influence, however. It can also be the by-product of busyness. We pastors pour out emotional energy on many fronts: weddings, funerals, baby dedications, Sunday sermons, study, counseling, and plenty of other ministry-related issues. All of this work can take us away from the deep well of rich friendships. Giving always seems more spiritual than receiving. Still, we remember that when Jesus said that "it is more blessed to give than to receive" (Acts 20:35), he was talking about helping the poor. He was not diminishing our need to receive encouragement, love, and admiration from others. But for a pastor, being on the receiving end may seem foreign.

Loneliness is not a badge of sacrifice but of pride. We fear letting people get to know us. We fear being needy and admitting we could use encouragement. We think we can do this alone, which is why we find ourselves in lonely situations.

I'm not saying that you should never be alone. Because of all the people demands, there will be times where you just want some space. Just be careful. Too much space over an extended period of time is not healthy. We were not designed to be loners. I am aware that there are different personality types and some are, by nature, more private than others, but Scripture is quite clear that we were made for relationships. We are to "confess your sins to each other" (James 5:16)—this is healthy! Who in your life can you trust to point out your blind spots? Your wife can see some of them, but not all. If we don't have close relationships where honest dialogue can take place, we are missing a major piece of spiritual real estate. Many folks have come alongside me and lovingly pointed out areas that need improvement. I thank God for them.

Be open and teachable. Invite people into your world who will give you an honest perspective about how you come across. This can only help your ministry.

Losing the Comparison Game

From time to time, we pastors will meet with others who have the same calling in life. We naturally have an affinity for those who understand our mission and the daily challenges that come with it. We are able to relate to and encourage one another the way people in the workforce seek out those with similar careers. Though pastors may not meet one another after work at the local watering hole, we do enjoy sharing the blessings and challenges of ministry with one another. If nothing else, it feels good to know that you are not the only one facing tough situations.

Before long, however, you find a pastor who seems like he is able to weather any storm and has such confidence in God that you wonder if you missed the faith boat when it left the harbor. He's the one with the fastest growing church in town and who preaches all over the country because he is in such demand. And you are not. His church baptized two hundred people last week; you don't even have that many who attend. These are battles most of us face.

You will also find that each pastor is prone to a different set of faith challenges. For example, some pastors battle with doctrinal issues and find themselves in a tangled web of theological underbrush. They tend to read scholarly works and may be frustrated that great minds can so often disagree. They can become concerned because they feel they lack the scholarship of those whom they read—who are in conflict with others they read. How can we be expected to know what the text says when those we read are not in harmony with one another?

Other pastors have different obstacles. I happen to be one of those people who always has to trace everything to its logical conclusion. I just can't seem to leave well enough alone.

Here is an example of how I think: Have you ever wondered why, in many churches, the guy in the pulpit has to have formal training and is given thirty minutes of airtime, while the Sunday school teacher, with no formal training, is given an hour? The person with zero training is given twice the time to minister as the one with a doctorate.

This same line of thinking goes into other areas of the church. For instance, you have probably heard something like this: "I can't stand these Bible studies where the leader asks each person what they think the text means. This is just a pooling of ignorance!" It might be, but the person who raises such an objection would, in the next breath, encourage each of those people in that study to have a private devotional time. What is the difference? There is no one looking over their shoulder interpreting the text for them. Besides that, if you had a bunch of scholars in a Bible study and asked them what the text says, though you would no longer be pooling ignorance, you would be pooling conflicting scholarship.

I also find myself conflicted between delivering a careful exegesis of the text and bringing practical truth. What is a healthy church in the eyes of God? Is it a body of well-taught believers who have a strong grip on theology, or is it a body of believers who have a great love for one another? We should hope to find a balance, certainly, but that seems to be a rare combination. Pastors struggle with such issues, though many of your questions will be different than mine.

Even if you are not tempted to spend time comparing yourself to other pastors, you might struggle within your own staff or ministry team. Pastors do not always find it easy to let go of the territory we have prized over the years. But if we are to stay focused in our work, we must be willing to relinquish some areas of ministry and trust it to others. "But Mike," you say, "what if they do not do as good a job as I have done?" We fear they might ruin something in which we have invested much time. That is a natural concern, but perhaps an even greater concern is that they may do a much *better* job, which might even make us look bad. These are issues of the heart and become mirrors that reveal the idols from within. If our own glory becomes more important to us than God's glory, then we will need times of refinement.

I knew a pastor many years ago who fired any staff member who became more popular than he was. If the youth ministry flourished, it was "bye bye" youth pastor. This happened over and over. *He* needed the praise of his people. Remember that God will often put us in difficult situations to reveal our true character. Pastors need refining, perhaps more so than those under our care. If you and I are to be sufficient for the task at hand, then we must release certain areas of ministry to those who are in a better position to serve. Kingdom work is a team effort. Jealousy has ruined many a church, and the pastor—of all people—must rid himself of this inner master.

The Bible says that being jealous is a "worldly" problem (1 Cor. 3:3). So, if this is a problem for you, then repent and admit to God the war within your own soul. Thank him for those he has gifted who can do certain jobs better than you can. Build a team of people who pull one another together, not apart. Publicly compliment those who come alongside you and seem to shine more brightly than you do. Genuine appreciation will replace feelings of jealousy, and grace will show up in ways you could never have imagined.

The apostle Paul himself felt inadequate, which is why he thanked God for those the Lord brought into his life to help shoulder the load (Rom. 16). People who are more gifted than we are in certain areas are not a threat. They are gifts from God.

Another area that may cause some to stumble is trying to live up to our own expectations and the expectations of our congregation. Many pastors agonize over the endless suggestions that come from members of the flock. They may claim to represent many others within the body, so you had better listen to them or else attendance and giving will drop. As the fear of man begins to set in, we start imagining the worst of scenarios. Many of us struggle with our inadequacies as it is, so we may look at the big picture and realize that far more is expected of us than we can hope to deliver. After all, since we are the ones who dispense wisdom at the weekend services, it only stands to reason that we should know what to do in all situations.

Nothing strikes more fear in my heart than to hear these words at a leadership meeting: "So Mike, you're the pastor; what do you think?" Suddenly, the onus is on me. What I say carries greater weight because of my position. What I say may set us on a collision course, yet I don't want to defer, lest I disagree with the course that another might set. These weighty matters cause sleepless nights—our decisions affect souls for eternity, don't they?

We may also feel the weight of expectations for our personal lives. What do people think of my children? Will one of my kids cause me heartache and embarrassment? Will I be judged as not being a good father? What if it leaks out that my marriage is not all that it should be? What about the way I handle my finances? Do people think I'm friendly enough?

As we try to understand ourselves, we will find that we are in far more need of grace than we could ever imagine. We must back away and take a good, hard look at what Scripture says about us and about the church. Then we need to preach truths to ourselves. "The one who calls you is faithful, and he will do it" (1 Thess. 5:24). Remind yourself daily of that promise. If God's grace was sufficient for Paul (2 Cor. 12:9), then will it be sufficient for you? Do we really believe that this is Christ's church and that he will build it (Matt. 16:18)?

Some of you may be saying, "I have believed all these things and preached those truths to myself, but nothing has worked." You feel your church is caving in. People are leaving and finances are drying up. There is conflict and your soul is spent. You have spent hours in prayer, but there is seemingly no relief. You detest going to the church office because the undercurrent of turmoil is palpable and you want to avoid anyone who reminds you of the present pain. Have faith.

He Will Do It

Now here is some food for thought and some encouragement for when discouragement comes. A moment ago, I advised you to preach 1 Thessalonians 5:24 to yourself: "The one who calls you is faithful, and he will do it." The fact that God not only calls us but that *he will do it* is a mighty promise. But think about this: Do we do the work of ministry? Does God? Or is this a cooperative effort?

Let's look at a few passages that dive into that tension, and I trust you will come away with renewed hope in your calling. In Exodus 3, we find God telling Moses that he (God) will rescue the children of Israel from Egyptian bondage while at the same time telling Moses that he (Moses) will deliver them (Exod. 3:8–10).

In the New Testament, we see the apostle Paul claiming that "I have been crucified with Christ and I no longer live, but Christ lives in me. The life I now live in the body, I live by faith in the Son of God, who loved me and gave himself for me" (Gal. 2:20). So who is living this life, Paul or Christ? Then in Colossians 1:29, Paul states, "To this end I also labor, striving according to His working which works in me mightily" (NKJV). Who is laboring, Paul or Christ?

This dichotomy shows up all throughout Scripture and may very well fall into the category of "how unsearchable are His judgments and His ways past finding out!" (Rom. 11:33 NKJV). Explaining how all of this works is not the issue. The issue is trusting that God will work in and through us. As you read, you may be facing a seemingly insurmountable obstacle. There are walls too high to climb simply by willing ourselves to do it. There are hurdles that will not be cleared by our own strength. Sooner or later, we will face "parting of the Red Sea" caliber challenges that wear down our souls. We will face giants looming and feel inadequate for the battle ahead. But so did Joshua and Caleb and David, who had to confront literal giants. Moses, Paul, and everyone in between found themselves with burdens too great to bear. Yet as we look at the whole picture of their lives, we see the invisible hand of the Lord guiding in such a way as to fulfill his good purposes.

So take a good, hard look at what you are facing. Admit your complete inability to make it on your own. See yourself as part of God's master plan, and know that he will succeed in bringing to pass all that he desires. Then ask yourself whether your fear, jealousy, worry, or desire for control are hindering the progress. It may seem contradictory that I have clearly stated that the Lord will have his way while also implying that we can slow down his plan. I don't have time to dissect the nuances of God's sovereignty and providence in this book, but we are given clear revelation that God's people do play a significant role in his redemptive purposes. Take joy, Pastor, that you are his vessel.

CHAPTER 12

THE PASTOR AND ENDURING

Through the years I have had good friends say to me, "Mike, we want you to finish well." I have always appreciated such sentiments. These are people who care enough for me to make certain I don't trip before reaching the finish line. They are watching my back, since they have seen too many evangelical figures make the headlines because of a moral or ethical failure. They have seen the devastating effects that a pastor's sin can have on the local church—and the church at large—not to mention the pastor's family, who must live with this indelible stain on their reputation for the rest of their lives. It doesn't end there, either. The consequences snowball down through the ages as future generations hear about the hypocrisy of their great-grandfather as he made a mockery of the gospel he preached. If that doesn't make you nervous, it should. The fallout of sin is greater than we could ever imagine (just ask King David).

What does finishing well look like? That is a question I asked myself several years ago as I pondered the exhortations to run the race in such a way as to get "the prize" (1 Cor. 9:24). Does that mean there are a series of hurdles a pastor must clear to make it into the Pastoral Hall of Fame? Are points given based on the number of converts, baptisms, or dollars under our church leadership? The race is not just for pastors, of course. The words "well done, good and faithful servant" (Matt. 25:21) will be heard by many who have no official ministry title.

Having given this much thought over the years, I decided that finishing well means *finishing with the fewest regrets*. It means coming to the end of your life knowing that Christ was exalted over the years, regardless of how much money you raised or how many people came through the doors of your church. I desire such a freedom from regret for myself and all pastors.

So how do you know if you're running well—or even running in the right direction? The answer to that may look different depending on how far along you are in your pastoral course. But whether you are just starting out or the finish line is in sight, it is always a good time to assess how you are doing. And it is never too late to pick up the pace.

Let's look at this in three different stages of your life as a pastor.

Stage 1: Imagination

The young pastor looks into the future and sees explosive growth in his church, based on his great expository and visionary skills. I call this the *imagination stage.* If you are starting out as a church planter or have taken over an existing church, here are a few pitfalls you will want to avoid:

1. **Remember that all members of the body are a gift to the church.** We must never see ourselves as better than others in the body, even though we carry a great responsibility. There is only one Savior, and you are not him. Enter with humility, and you will avoid being humbled.

2. **Give all your expectations to the Lord.** It is his church and not yours. He may call you to preach to thousands, to hundreds, or to tens. Your writing might become a *New York Times* best seller. It may end up as an insert for the church bulletin. God will be glorified in either.

3. **Build your team around humility, not talent.** It took me years to get this right. If your staff and lay leaders lack humility, even the most talented person can become more than a thorn in your side. This is not to downplay talent or giftedness, but if those are mixed with pride, you are in for a long

haul of sleepless nights, awkward meetings, and tension on every side of your ministry.

4. **Don't brush small problems under the carpet.** This is one of my greatest regrets. I love to make peace but run from conflict. That has cost me dearly. You don't need to chase down every concern, but when you sense something is rotten in the state of Denmark, it is time to check it out. Stamping out a small spark is easier than putting out a raging fire. I have the burn marks to prove it.

5. **Stay in touch with your people and your team.** The people in your congregation will keep you in touch with reality, and your team will help address the issues.

6. **Decide early on how you will allocate your time.** Some pastors spend thirty to thirty-five hours per week preparing for Sunday, while others may only spend eight to ten so they can devote more time to hospital visits, counseling, or discipling. Scripture gives us limited direction here, but such decisions must be made based on where you have been called to pastor and your own personality. No matter how much you do, there are things that will be left undone. You must prioritize.

7. **Keep careful records of all your personal meetings.** You may need them later. I have never been good at this, to my own detriment. Memory fades, but notes do not.

8. **Develop good relationships with those in leadership and those outside.** This will give you balance in how you perceive the ministry. Church members often see things very differently than those "in the know." Leadership can't always see the forest for the trees, and those in the pews can't always see the trees for the forest. As with eyesight, both eyes are needed for proper depth of field. Don't be a one-eyed church.

9. **Seek wisdom and direction from older pastors.** They have been around the block a few times and know where the loose manhole covers are. Talk to them and lean on their experience.

Stage 2: Experience

The second stage of pastoral ministry is often plagued with second guessing. You may tend to look back on your ministry and focus on the failures. That is the enemy's calling card. He loves to keep you distracted with questions like, "Where did I go wrong with this church? Why are people so difficult? Why can't they be like me? Have I been faking it this whole time? Did I misread God's calling? Should I have been an engineer?"

Instead, I love to sift my thoughts through Philippians, where Paul is writing from jail, encouraging readers to be joyful. That's irony behind bars, and it shows a heart consumed more by what God is doing than his own situation. Here are a few other ways you can keep yourself from running aground during this season of ministry.

1. **Take inventory of your history as a pastor thus far.** What have you done well and what could you improve? Where do you tend to bear the most fruit? At my twenty-year mark we had a large celebration commemorating two decades of God's faithfulness. I had a chance to see the people whose lives had been changed, but I was reminded that this had never been "The Mike Minter Show." Hundreds of people over those years were a part of the work that God was doing.

2. **Ask yourself what midcourse corrections need to be made.** Seek out some honest friends who have observed you through the years. They know your blind spots. I have had dear brothers with the courage to tell me that I was running on fumes and that my messages were lacking depth. They knew I was tired. Ministry can drain you. I also

turned in my resignation once in the early 2000s, after we lost close to one thousand people to a local megachurch within a few months. Talk about ministry trauma! I felt like I was failing. One of the elders threw my letter in the trash and said, "We have work to do." Deep in my heart, I knew I was called to stay the course, but the pain of loss was difficult to bear. I was certain the ship would capsize. It didn't, and here we are many years later. Be honest with yourself throughout your years of ministry.

3. **Take note of the cultural changes that have taken place.** Moral, ethical, and technological manifestations are interpreted differently by generations and religious backgrounds. Every pastor should have knowledge of the cultural narratives pulsing through our society. You can get left in the dust if you are not aware of them. They can slip in unannounced and, before you know it, your ministry is no longer relevant. As someone once said, "There are those who make things happen, those who watch things happen, and those who wonder what happened." Don't miss the train on this.

4. **Spend time with the younger people in your church, and find out how they view**

life. This will be an eye-opener. Obviously, this can be done at any stage, but after a decade or two, it is a good time to test the waters of youth. They are living in a different world. That wasn't true when I first came to Reston. Back then, it seemed that generations were separated by inches. Today, the internet has separated them by miles. I have loved sitting down with teens and asking them what life is like in school and what battles they are facing. Believe me, they will be up front about it.

5. **Be honest enough with yourself to discern whether you never really had a heart for this thing called "ministry."** This is a tough one, but it needs to be addressed before you build up decades of regret. Is there a fire in your belly for teaching God's Word and caring for people? If it was there once, then get counsel on how to reignite it. The enemy loves to create doubt and question our calling. If, on the other hand, you just thought this was a way to put food on the table, it's time to go before your leadership and seek their counsel. Resigning is not *always* the worst thing in the world. And if you are not called to ministry, it might be the best thing for your family.

Stage 3: The Rearview Mirror

Stage three is for the pastor who has managed to survive twenty-five years and longer. I will refer to this as the *rearview mirror* stage. In this stage, there is a greater longing for heaven and a desire to leave a legacy for your family, church, and friends. It can be the most profitable time in all your life. It is a time to gather with those you love and tell tales of bygone years. It is a time to laugh and see life through the lens of wisdom and experience.

As the name suggests, this phase of ministry also becomes a time of reflection, which can engender regrets, sometimes even leading to depression or deep sadness. Questions may arise like, "Why didn't I lead better or spend more time with my people?" I, for one, certainly wish I had been better at counseling. The list of questions and doubts surface like a whale coming up for air.

Obviously, we can't erase past failures, be they ethical, moral, or just lacking wisdom. Finishing well means living in daily repentance. Finishing well means maintaining a "conscience clear before God and man" (Acts 24:16). This was a supreme desire of the apostle Paul, who had persecuted the church and must have had many regrets in mind when he referred to himself as "chief" among sinners (1 Tim. 1:15 NKJV).

Why did God see David as "a man after his own heart" (1 Sam. 13:14) but reject Saul who seemed to have fewer sins recorded? It is because David repented wholeheartedly (as expressed in Psalm 32 and Psalm 51), yet Saul persisted in his hatred of David without repentance, making excuses for his disobedience.

Chuck Swindoll once said, "It is never too late to start doing what is right."[4] That is a very wise statement. No matter how old you are as a pastor (or retired pastor), you have time to make things right. A clear conscience is a key component of finishing well. No pillow is soft enough to soothe a guilty conscience.

As I said earlier, finishing well is finishing with the fewest regrets. Are there any loose ends regarding relationships that need to be healed? Are there people who have served faithfully and need to be thanked? Leave no stone unturned and you will finish well.

CHAPTER 13

THE PASTOR AND HOLY PLEASURES

About fifteen years ago, I was reading through Romans and came upon a very familiar text: "For the kingdom of God is not a matter of eating and drinking, but of righteousness, peace and joy in the Holy Spirit" (Rom. 14:17). The great beauty of Scripture is that it is alive, and we are often introduced to a fresh insight that previously had been hidden. The expression "joy in the Holy Spirit" struck me. What exactly does that mean? What does it look like when I am experiencing it? I began to look back over my ministry and thought about all the people who had been changed by the Word going forth. I began thinking about the many who had been called into missions and the churches that had been planted around the world because of so many faithful people, the ones willing to go and the ones who sent them. I pondered the prodigals who had returned and marriages that had been healed. I couldn't help but think of the young people who found their spouses at church. Before long, my mind was filled with emotion.

In the process, I came up with this definition of *joy*: Joy is the inner spiritual confidence that God's grace is sufficient to see me through my earthly pilgrimage.

We have sailed through some pretty rough waters in this book, so I think that it would be fitting to end by considering some "holy pleasures." These are the times when God meets us with an overabundance of his grace, when God surprises us with his Spirit, and when God is doing things behind the scenes of which we are completely unaware. We all have experiences like this, where we truly feel the joy of God's Spirit. I want to share with you some holy pleasures from my years of ministry—they are wonderful gifts from God.

A few years ago, I received a letter from a young lady who said she visited RBC back when we were meeting in a local school. She said, "I was invited by one of my classmates and only attended once because my family moved to Colorado right after I graduated." She went on to say that when she heard the gospel, she called upon the Lord to save her and is now married to a youth pastor. She just wanted to say "thanks." *That* was a holy pleasure.

We once had a rebellious young man in our church who eventually came to the Lord and later went into missions. Having reached a tribal group in Northern Thailand, he returned to the States with some of his new converts. He brought them to an RBC service and had them give their testimonies as he translated. They thanked RBC for loving them enough to send a missionary into their tribe to preach Christ. I cannot describe the emotion we all felt. Here were three men we had never met, who lived thousands of miles from Virginia, telling us about the power of the gospel, which they heard from a man who used to wander far from the fold of God. *That* was a holy pleasure.

Then there was the young man jogging past our church one Sunday morning who decided to stop in and see what was happening. That very morning, he passed from death unto life and eventually came on staff. We in ministry live for such holy pleasures.

After preaching one Sunday morning, a lady walked up to me after the service and said she wanted to talk to me. I told her to call the office and set up a time. She said, "No, I want to talk now." I informed her that I had another service to preach and there wasn't time. She then said, "I'm an atheist and I want to talk now." I said, "Sit down; we need to talk."

I opened the conversation by asking, "Why are you here if you are an atheist?" She went on to tell me about the divorce she was going through and how some members of our body were helping her in this difficult time. She couldn't understand the love of those people who would receive nothing in return. I firmly looked at her and told her she wasn't an atheist but was someone in need of the truth. I went over the gospel very carefully, and she burst into tears and called upon the Lord to save her. I was skeptical about the genuineness of her conversion until she came back the next week with Bible in hand, had already devoured a Christian book, and had witnessed to her mother. *That* was certainly a holy pleasure.

My brother and his wife spent many years as missionaries in Papua New Guinea. After a number of years learning the language and eventually giving the gospel to the entire tribe, many were converted. We asked my brother to share with the congregation, by way of a phone call, how the gospel had been presented to this people group. We patched in the conversation through our speaker system as our body listened to my brother relate what happened. We could hardly contain ourselves. RBC had spent thousands of dollars to send my brother and his family to this distant land, and now there is a thriving indigenous church with a copy of the New Testament in their own language. We had no idea what the results would be, but reflecting back I can see that this was a holy pleasure of great magnitude.

There are also difficult holy pleasures that are pleasures nonetheless. Several years ago, Trey, a man in his early fifties, was diagnosed with cancer. At first, it seemed to be easily curable. But later, we received news that it had spread to his lungs. He battled valiantly for two years, eventually succumbing to the disease. Prior to his departure from this world, he wanted to make every moment count. He agreed to be a part of an Easter outreach at RBC, where we performed some skits, interspersed with testimonies of people who were experiencing resurrection power in the midst of suffering. Though feeling very weak, Trey went to all the rehearsals and stood for five straight nights proclaiming the power of God to many lost people. As his passing grew near, he emailed me his memorial service program to get my thoughts. His wife called for the elders to come over on a Monday evening to have a final word of prayer for Trey and say our goodbyes. He was under hospice care and could barely whisper. We prayed for Trey and as we started to leave, he motioned to us that he wanted to stand up and hug us. His son and future son-in-law came in and lifted him up. We all went over and hugged Trey. One of our elders looked him in the eye and said, "I'm not going to say goodbye, but see ya later." Trey passed away two days later, and I had the great privilege to proclaim the gospel to about five hundred people who were teammates from his college football years, neighbors, coworkers, and extended family. Though difficult, this was a most holy pleasure.

During one of our men's retreats, I was able to hear the testimonies of men as we were all assigned to tables, approximately eight men per table. One of the first things we were tasked with was to tell our stories. Three of the men that were at my table I had known for years, but I had never heard how they came to know Christ. As it turned out, all three of these men said they came to faith under my preaching. Now let me pause for a moment and make something very clear: The gospel—not my ability to preach—is "the power of God that brings salvation" (Rom. 1:16). I was humbled to hear their stories and to see how mighty the gospel is.

One of the men was a rocket scientist. He told the story of how his wife brought him to our church. As they pulled into the parking lot that Sunday, he saw our sign—Reston Bible Church. When he found out it was a "Bible church," he insisted that they leave because he was not going to set foot in a place where they believed the Bible. His wife said, "We are here, so let's go in and if we don't like it, we don't have to come back." He reluctantly agreed. They took a seat, and he sat with his arms folded. Would you like to guess what I happened to preach on that weekend? "The Divine Authority of Scripture." It was a message on apologetics. He told me later that it was like a sword that went through his proud heart. I always give the gospel each week, and when I did that week, he bowed his head and called upon Christ to save him. He later served on our mission committee. *That* was a holy pleasure.

I can't tell you the number of times I have heard people tell me about their reluctance to come to church but, after attending, the Holy Spirit worked mightily in their heart and they came to know Christ. I'm reminded of a lady who sent her son to our Awana program, where he would faithfully learn his memory verses. His mother would help him each week to memorize the verses. She was an unbeliever but felt her son needed some kind of spiritual training. One evening as she was helping him memorize Ephesians 2:8–9, she realized that this was just as much for her as it was for him, and she called upon the Lord and was converted. *That* was a holy pleasure.

One Sunday morning during a baptismal service, the wife of our children's director gave her testimony. I was standing in the back of the sanctuary, expecting to hear how her conversion must have taken place in Brazil, where she was from. Her husband was not far along in his faith when he married her, and she was an unbeliever. They started attending RBC, much against her will. In her testimony that morning, she began to tell of her dislike for her husband, Mike, because he was trying to convert her. She then said, "After we started attending RBC, I found another Mike I didn't like." The congregation burst into laughter because it was a not-so-subtle jab at me. She went on to tell of how she would come week after week in anger toward the gospel. After a year, however, her heart began to soften and she eventually trusted Christ. Mike eventually came on staff as our children's director and now serves as pastor of family life. He and his wife also operate a thriving ministry of evangelism in Brazil. They are having a profound impact for the kingdom. *That* was a holy pleasure!

Some of these holy pleasures were put into motion well before I even came to Christ. Here is one of my favorites: When I was in high school, one of my closest friends was a young guy named Mac. We were the best of friends, but as we grew older, we went our separate ways and soon lost touch. That was around 1963. I came to know Christ in 1970 and in the ensuing years had not heard anything about Mac or his whereabouts. In 1990, I got a call from Mac, who was living in California at the time, and he informed me that he was going to be in the Northern Virginia area and wanted to grab some time with me. I was eager for the opportunity to witness to my old friend. I knew he had no spiritual interest, unless something had dramatically changed in his life, as it had in mine. Over lunch I gave Mac my testimony and he had that look on his face that said, "I'm glad you found what you have been looking for, but I'm not really interested." We moved on to another subject and parted ways, not knowing if I would ever see or hear from Mac again.

Eight or ten years after that reunion, I received a phone call from Mac right in the middle of dinner. I slipped away from the table and we had some "How's the family?" small talk. He informed me that everything was going great but something was missing. He then said something to the effect of "Mike, do you remember when we had lunch a few years ago and you told me about your faith in Christ?"

"Yes," I said.

He asked me to tell him again what I had told him then. After our conversation he wanted to know what to do. I said, "When we hang up, I want you to go to some quiet place and admit your desperate need for Christ to save you." He did and is now a lay pastor in a local church and calls me from time to time to tell me of his spiritual growth. That was a holy pleasure years in the making.

On my yearly trips to the Amazon, one of my great joys is to eat with the pastors and their wives and get all the news from the past year. A few years ago, I was seated next to Pastor Cosme and his wife, with my interpreter across the table. I inquired of his ministry over the past year. He replied that it had been a great year, in spite of the fact that both his church and his house were washed away during the rainy season, and he almost lost his leg from a stingray injury. (The hospital was more than one hour away by boat!) I looked at Mike, my interpreter, and said, "I don't think Pastor Cosme understood my question. That doesn't sound like a good year." Mike repeated the question, and the answer came back the same with a brief footnote. The pastor said he can always rebuild the church or his home, but he knows his home in heaven will never be washed away.

How many of us react that way to life's challenges? Not me, that's for sure. I complain when we are out of coffee creamer! But that's not the end of the story. Each year, the American team alternates between serving communion and washing the feet of the pastors and their wives. That evening, Pastor Cosme was in my group. As I knelt down to wash his feet, I saw the scar where the stingray drove its poisonous spike through his foot.

My eyes filled with tears and the first verse that came to my mind, which I repeated loudly, was: "How beautiful are the feet of those who bring good news!" (Rom. 10:15). That was such a holy pleasure.

I suspect my greatest holy pleasures have come through my family. I have a wife who has prayed for me through the most difficult of times. Kay has a much simpler faith than mine. I tend to analyze theology to death, and she just trusts that all will be well. It usually is.

My daughter Kelly is our oldest and writes women's Bible studies for Lifeway as well as travels and speaks. She is our most driven child when it comes to getting things done. If there is a boulder in the way, she will have it removed one way or the other. She has the gift of wisdom, and many rely on her for it.

Megan is the head of the HR department of a small company. If you just want some loving care, Megan is the shoulder to cry on. She is unflappable, laid-back, and is loved by all. "Sweet" may be the best way to describe her.

Katie will push every envelope there is to push. She prides herself in being a firecracker, and that is an understatement. Her home is filled with neighborhood kids who love to just sit and chat. Her laugh can be heard a mile away. Her many health issues have been a challenge, but I have never seen anyone fight harder.

David completes the clan. As many have said to me, "If you don't like David Minter, you're the problem." He is very laid-back, but he is filled with wisdom and distributes it with grace. He is a natural peacemaker who makes everyone comfortable in his presence.

Katie and David are both married to wonderful spouses and we have six grandchildren who keep us hopping. My wife and I are blessed people. Our greatest joy—and a holy pleasure—is that all our kids are mature in Christ.

These pleasures are gifts of God's grace that help keep us energized to stay the course. We are not entitled to hear how our witness is bearing fruit, but in God's economy, he may give us glimpses of the ways he is using us. We get the blessing, while he gets all the glory. All such holy pleasures should humble us and make us more dependent upon him and amazed at his goodness. We can't manufacture such pleasures, but we can rejoice when God brings them our way.

The ultimate holy pleasure must be Christ himself. Let us say with the apostle Paul, "But whatever were gains to me I now consider loss for the sake of Christ. What is more, I consider everything a loss because of the surpassing worth of knowing Christ Jesus my Lord" (Phil. 3:7–8). We must see Christ as the "Alpha and the Omega," the beginning and the end (Rev. 1:8). We must realize that without him we "can do nothing" (John 15:5). Our hope is that God would make us "instruments for special purposes, made holy, useful to the Master and prepared to do any good work" (2 Tim. 2:21). To the degree that we lack this understanding, we will trust in and delight in other things. We must see Christ as all-sufficient, and when we do, we will discover those holy pleasures.

THE JOY OF STAYING THE COURSE

It has been my supreme joy to have gone on this journey with you. Ministry is difficult work, but it is the most rewarding work in the world.

At the twentieth anniversary of RBC, we rented out a large hotel ballroom to celebrate what the Lord had done over the years. My mom and dad attended, and it was a thrill to have them in the front row. After the event was over, my dad pulled me aside and said, "You have accomplished far more than I have in life." I was stunned. I remember disagreeing with him, but that was not up for discussion.

My dad fought for our country in WWII and the Korean War. He was skipper of the aircraft carrier *Intrepid* and Commandant and Superintendent of the United States Naval

Academy. He retired as a three-star Admiral. What could he have possibly meant by such words? I pulled aside a retired admiral in our congregation and asked what he thought about my dad's comment. Here is roughly how he replied: "What your dad accomplished for his country could never be taken lightly. But I think he realizes that what you have been called to counts for eternity."

My point in sharing this story is that we pastors (along with all believers) are "sojourners and pilgrims" in this world (1 Pet. 2:11 NKJV). And as Hebrews tells us, Abraham "was looking forward to the city with foundations, whose architect and builder is God" (11:10). We must develop and maintain an eternal perspective as we walk through this very strange land. The seas can be rough, but much like Jesus's promise to his disciples, we will make it to the other shore. Travel uphill. Swim against the moral current, and feel the splinters of going against the grain of this present evil age—whichever metaphor fits you best—our purpose is to invite those "living in darkness" (Luke 1:79) to enter the "kingdom of light" (Col. 1:12). Could there be a greater calling?

A number of years ago, I had a dear friend who could tell whenever I was near rock bottom. We would go to lunch, and I would pour my heart out about how difficult church problems were and how I wasn't sure I could endure much longer. He always answered the same way: "You are concerned about the church as if it were yours. It's not. It belongs to Christ and Christ alone. So why do you take on his responsibilities? Why do you live in the fear of man and future problems? They don't belong to you."

I realize this may sound like we have no responsibility and we just cast it all on Jesus. But the truth is that we are only responsible to carry out *our* calling; we leave the results to the Head of the church. As I look back, I can see his hand guiding Reston Bible Church every step of the way. From moving six times over the years, to giving millions toward world missions, to sending many from our body off to foreign fields, to watching prodigal sons and daughters return, to seeing marriages restored, to seeing lives changed—it has all been by his grace and for his glory.

Pastor, I urge you not to simply "hang in there" as you persevere in ministry. Instead, be assured of God's mighty presence and power to fulfill what he has called us to do. You are not in this alone.

I leave you with these final thoughts. You, my friend, are a servant of the Most High God, the ruler of heaven and earth. He is sovereignly in charge of all things in heaven and earth. He will do what he desires, and nothing—and no one, including you—will thwart his plans. I have to remind myself of these truths daily, and you will, too. These are not merely words on a page, but they are promises from the King of kings and Lord of lords. Rest on them. Rely on them and stay the course.

> May God himself, the God of peace, sanctify you through and through. May your whole spirit, soul and body be kept blameless at the coming of our Lord Jesus Christ. The one who calls you is faithful, and he will do it. (1 Thess. 5:23–24)

NOTES

1. J. C. Ryle, *Practical Religion* (1879; repr., Germany: Outlook Verlag, 2018), 80.

2. "Taking God's Name in Vain?" BibleProject podcast, March 19, 2020, https://bibleproject.com/podcast/taking-gods -name-vain/.

3. A. W. Tozer, *Man: The Dwelling Place of God*, rev. ed. (Chicago: Moody Publishers, 1997).

4. Charles Swindoll, *Day by Day* (Nashville: Thomas Nelson, 2005), https://www.oneplace.com/devotionals/todays-insight -from-chuck-swindoll/day-by-day-july-13-2011-11653226.html.